FROM

ACROSS THE TIAN SHAN TO LOB-NOR.

COLONEL N. PREJEVALSKY,
AUTHOR OF "TRAVELS IN MONGOLIA."

TRANSLATED BY
E. DELMAR MORGAN, F.R.G.S.
MEM. OF THE IMP. RUSS. GEOGR. SOC.

INCLUDING NOTICES OF THE LAKES OF CENTRAL ASIA.

With Introduction

By Sl . T. DOUGLAS FORSYTH, C.B., K.C.S.I.

1879.

PREFACE.

THE favourable reception accorded two years ago to " Travels in Mongolia," and the interest which still attaches to the countries of Central Asia induce me to publish an English version of Colonel Prejevalsky's travels to Lob-nor, the more readily that no European hitherto has visited it in modern times.

That Colonel Prejevalsky's narrative is so brief is accounted for by the great physical prostration from which its author has been suffering, the effect of hardship and exposure in desert and swamp, necessitating his giving up for the time all literary work and taking complete rest at his estate in the government of Smolensk.

Soon after this translation was begun, Baron von Richthofen's lecture, delivered before the Berlin Geographical Society, on the results of Prejevalsky's journey appeared in print. So interesting and suggestive a commentary from the pen of one of the first geographers of the day could not fail to attract the attention of the public. I therefore lost no time in communicating with the Baron through the kind instrumentality of Colonel Yule, and received from him a prompt reply to my request for further particulars, together with two map-tracings illustrating his views. The following extracts are from Baron Richthofen's letter to Colonel Yule. "I send you two tracings; one of them is a true copy of the Chinese map, the other is made from a sketch which I constructed to-day, and on which I tried to put down the Chinese topography together with that of Prejevalsky. It appears evident—1, that Prejevalsky travelled by the ancient road to a point south of the true Lop-noor; 2, that long before he reached this point he found the river courses quite different from what they had been formerly; and, 3, that following one of the new rivers which flows due south by a new road, he reached the two sweet-water lakes, one of which answers to the ancient Khas-omo. I use the word 'new' merely by way of comparison with the state of things in Kien-long's time when the map was made. It appears that the Chinese map shows the Khas lake too far north to cover the Kara-Koshun. The bifurcation of the roads south of the lake nearly resembles that which is marked by Prejevalsky . . .

"Orography is the weakest point of Chinese maps. Where a mountain is marked there is certain to be one; but it is impossible to say whether it be high or low, steep or rounded, continuous or isolated. The boundary, however, of hill country towards level land can in most cases be approximately traced. In the present case it [i. e. the hill country] is about as far distant from Khas-omo as the Altyn-tagh is from the Kara-Koshun."

Upon receiving this I wrote to Colonel Prejevalsky, asking him to furnish me with replies to Baron Richthofen's criticisms, so as to enable me to throw as much light as possible on the subject in the book I was preparing for the press. A translation of his answer will be found on pages 160—165 of the present volume.

In the meanwhile a paragraph appeared in the *Athenæum* of the 14th September from which I quote the following :—

"It would appear that the Russian traveller
Prejevalsky in his last remarkable journey in the
heart of Central Asia, did not explore Lob-nor at
all, as he claims to have done. Baron Ferdinand
von Richthofen, one of the first comparative
geographers of the day, has examined the account
of the journey more especially by the light of
Chinese literature, and proves, almost incontest-
ably to our thinking, that the true Lob-nor must
lie somewhere north-east of the so-called Kara-
Kotchun Lake discovered by Prejevalsky, and that
in all probability it is fed by an eastern arm
of the Tarim river. This, at all events, would
account for the remarkable diminution in bulk
undergone by the waters of that stream as they
proceed southward, which could not but strike an
attentive reader of the Russian explorer's narrative. The whole question is well worthy of further
investigation, and it is possible that Prejevalsky,
whom a recent telegram from St. Petersburg
reports as about to return to Central Asia, may
be enabled to elucidate it."

On reading this it seemed to me that the writer
had been a little too hasty in his conclusions, and
that Colonel Prejevalsky might suffer an injustice

were the statement allowed to pass without comment. I therefore wrote to the Editor of the *Athenæum*, saying that I thought the remarks contained in his paper were somewhat premature.

Having now given the substance of the controversy, I leave the reader to form his own conclusions, but whatever these may be, it is impossible to deny that a tribute of praise is due from geographers of all nations to Colonel Prejevalsky for the undaunted energy and perseverance shown by him in all that he has undertaken.

The article on Lakes Balkash and Ala-kul is taken from the best Russian authorities, whilst that on the Starovertsi may be of interest to the general reader.

In the map, Mr. Weller, of Red Lion Square, has incorporated all the most recent information procurable, and in the region round Kulja or Kuldja, the cartography has been corrected according to a Russian MS. map in the collection of the Royal Geographical Society compiled in 1872, from surveys taken on the spot.

E. DELMAR MORGAN.

15, ROLAND GARDENS, S.W.
October, 1878.

CONTENTS.

a

CHAPTER III.

APPENDIX.

LAKE BALKASH.

LAKE ALA-KUL.

THE STAROVERTSI.

INTRODUCTORY REMARKS.

THE ancient history of this region is enveloped in considerable obscurity, but such glimpses as we are able to get at it through the stories of travellers, and the more or less fabulous tales of Mohammedan and other writers, are not without interest. For several centuries anterior to the Christian era it formed part of the empire of Turan, swayed by a long line of Scythian kings, who are referred to a common descent from the great family of Afrasyab.

The power of the Scythians appears to have been first broken by their western neighbours of Iran, and finally extinguished by the Macedonian conquest.

Syawush, about 580 B.C., fleeing from his father Kaikaos, crossed the Jyhoon, and sought refuge with the enemy of his family Afrasyab, who received him with kindness, and granted him an honourable asylum, and gave him his daughter, the beautiful Farangis, in marriage, with the provinces of Khoten and Chin as her dowry. Thither

B

Syawush retired with his bride, and settling at
Kung—probably Katak, the ruins of which now
exist near Lob, at twelve or sixteen days' journey
N.E. of Khoten, made it the capital of his government of Khoten and Chin, or, as it is usually
styled, Machin, which together comprised the
southern and eastern portion of the great basin
known as Eastern Turkestan.

The Bactrian kingdom of Soghdiana, invaded
by Alexander the Great about 300 B.C., was in its
turn overthrown by the invasion from the north
of the great Yuechi, or Tokhar, a branch of the
Tungun or Eastern Tartar people, who were
driven from their lands westward to the banks of
the Ili river just anterior to 200 B.C. by the Hiun-
guns or Huns, who conquered all the country from
the borders of China to the Volga, which they
held with varying success till their power over the
territory of Kashgar was broken, and they were
subjected to the Chinese about 94 A.D., in which
year the city of Kashgar was captured and annexed to China. For a long period this region
was under the rule of Chinese governors, but
gradually passed into the hands of petty independent princes, who were strong enough to throw
off their subjection to the empire, but who main-
tained a kind of allegiance, by sending periodical
embassies to China. In fact it is recorded that
such embassies from the extreme frontier states
were of very frequent occurrence, owing to the

facilities they afforded for smuggling merchandise through the frontier custom-houses. Their real object, as a mere cloak for purposes of trade, was soon recognized by the Chinese Government, and since the large number of foreigners entering the country in the train of the envoys gave rise to numerous disputes and much inconvenience, orders were issued for placing them under severe restrictions, and the operation of these regulations soon led to their discontinuance.

The most noted amongst these independent tribes seem to have been the Uighurs, whose chief, Satuk Boghra Khan, was the first Tartar prince who brought the Uighur people together as a nation. His empire extended from the shores of the Caspian to the Desert of Gobi, and the frontiers of China. He, moreover, introduced Islam into Eastern Turkestan towards the end of the tenth century.

The government of the Uighur passed into the hands of the Gurkhan of the Kara Khitai about the beginning of the thirteenth century.

These Uighurs were Turks, and were known to the Chinese as Hoei-hoei. In the second half of the eighth century and beginning of the ninth they were all powerful in Eastern Asia, and had their capital in Karakorum.

Nestorian Christianity was widely spread among them, and it was from the Nestorians that they doubtless derived their alphabet, which is founded on the Syriac. They taught letters to the Mongols, and were in early times the most cultivated race of Eastern Asia. From these people Jinghiz Khan borrowed a creed for his nomads, and letters in which to reduce their language to writing. The accountants, secretaries, and civil servants of both Jinghiz and his immediate successor were almost always taken from the same nationality. Their principal seat was Bishbalik (Ourumtsi).

The empire of Kara Khitai had been founded by a fugitive from China, a scion of the royal race of the Liau or Khitan dynasty, who escaped when that dynasty was overturned and ejected by the Yueche or Kin. Its sovereigns were styled the Gurkhans. They ruled immediately over the area known to the older geographers as Little Bucharia or Dzungaria, the Arslan Khans of Kashgar and the chiefs of the Uighurs being subject to them. In A.D. 1208 Kushluk, son of the chief of the Naimans, took refuge at their court. The Gurkhan was then a weak prince, the Naiman treacherous and crafty. He asked permission to collect the débris of his father's army, which was then scattered in the countries of Imil Kayalik and Bishbalik. The Gurkhan allowed him to do so, gave him the title of Gushluk Khan, and also gave him his daughter in marriage. He then collected an army, and, treacherously leaguing himself with the Khuarezm Shah, proceeded to overturn the power of his patron, and took Gurkhan prisoner, but left him the title of sovereign, which he only enjoyed for two years, and on his death Gushluk succeeded to the throne. He attacked and killed the Khan of Almalik, and ravaged the country of Kashgar. D'Ohsson says that having been brought up a Christian, he embraced Buddhism on the solicitation of his wife, a daughter of Gurkhan. Another account represents his wife as being Christian, whilst he remained a Buddhist.

Gushluk, though master of a wide empire, was unable to stand against the overwhelming force of Jinghiz Khan, whose general, Chepe Noyan, marched against Kashgar, in A.D. 1219, when Gushluk abandoned the city and fled across the Pamir to Badakshan, where he was captured and taken to Chepe, who had him beheaded. By the overthrow of Gushluk the Mongol dominion was extended over the whole country of Central Asia.

In the partition of the realm of Jinghiz Khan among his sons, the region of Eastern Turkestan, with Almalik as its capital, fell to the share of Jagatai, and his successors held it until Timur came with fire and sword, and made it part of his extensive empire. Then followed a confused period of dissensions between Mongol princes and Mongol tribes, during which we are led to believe that the civilization of Almalik and of the neighbouring cities of the valley of the Ili entirely disappeared. Regarding this city of Almalik, Colonel Yule gives the following information :—

"As early as the time of Jagatai himself, his summer camp was in the vicinity of Almalik, and when Hulagu was on the march from Karakorum to destroy the *mulahid* or 'assassins' in Persia (A.D. 1254) the princess regent Organah, widow of Kara Hulagu, grandson and successor of Jagatai, came out from Almalik to receive him with due honour." Hence it would appear that Almalik was one at least of the capitals from a very early date. In the following century, about 1330-34, we find Ibn Batuta observing that it was the proper capital of the kings of this dynasty, and that one of the charges brought against the Khan Tamarshin which led to his supersession was that he always remained in Mawar-al-nahr, and for four years running had not visited Almalik and the eastern dominions of his family.

Bishbalik-Ourumtsi was at first the head-quarters of the Khan, but it was afterwards transferred to Almalik.

Marignolli gives the following account of his visit to the great Khan :—

" We went to the first Emperor of the Tartar tribes and laid before him the letters which we bore, with certain pieces of cloth, a great war-horse, some strong liquor, and the Pope's presents. And after the winter was over, having been well fed, well clothed, loaded with handsome presents, and supplied by the king with horses and travelling expenses, we proceeded to Armalu, the capital of the Middle Empire. There we built a church, bought a piece of ground, dug wells, sung masses, and baptized several, preaching freely and openly, notwithstanding the fact that only the year before the Bishop and six other minor friars had there undergone for Christ's sake a glorious martyrdom."

During the supremacy of the descendants of Jinghiz, Jungaria, or Dzungaria, as all this country has been indifferently called, was the camping-ground of three powerful Mongol tribes—Choros, Hoshot, and Torgut, who subsequently took the name of Oirat, or *confederates*.

About the middle of the fourteenth century the Chinese threw off the Mongol yoke, and remained independent till the middle of the fifteenth century, when, after frequent wars, the Oirat defeated the Chinese in a very sanguinary battle, took the Emperor prisoner, and marched to the walls of Peking. Chance alone saved China. The Mongols retired to the steppes, the taitsi or Wuzeer Esen, who had killed his brother-in-law, the Khan, was assassinated, and the most brilliant period of the Oirat power was at an end. They were unable to maintain their influence in Mongolia, and for a century and a half almost disappeared from history.

We shall see a little farther on, how, in the present time, China has on another occasion been indebted to the assassin's hand for extrication from troubles on her western frontier, and how the death by violence of the Ameer Yakub Beg has been followed by the dissolution of his kingdom.

We now pass on to the reign of the Emperor Kien Long, who conquered Kashgar and Eastern Turkestan, and having slaughtered or expelled the whole Dzungarian population, repeopled the country of Dzungaria by sending military colonies from Manchuria, by deporting Chinese criminals, and by bringing agriculturists from Eastern Turkestan. For the purpose of keeping the country in order, the city of Ili, or what is called Manchu Kulja, was built as the seat of government, and was settled by Manchus. Six other forts were built.

It is owing to these wars and invasions, with their constant changes of population, and to the measures taken by the Chinese Government that the region of Kulja has its present curious mixture of races and peoples.

The settlers from Eastern Turkestan became known as Taranchis, literally agriculturists, or millet-sowers, from "taran," millet. (Schuyler's "Turkistan," ii. 168 seq.)

The military colonists were brought from Dauria, in North-West Mongolia, and consisted of Solons, who are still famous in all China for their skill in archery, and Sibos, a tribe on whose gratitude the Chinese Government could especially count, because at the accession of the Manchu dynasty they were freed from their slavery to the Mongols.

The country being secured in this way, it was perfectly safe for the Chinese to send there the Dzungars and the Oirat, who had previously sought their protection; and, subsequently, they also allowed many to come back who had fled from the massacres, and had taken refuge among the Kirghiz. These were further reinforced by the arrival of the Kalmuks, from Russia, in A.D. 1771, whose journey has been immortalized by De Quincey, in his "Flight of a Tartar Tribe." These Kalmuks were settled in the excellent pasture-grounds on the Kunges and the Tekes, where they still live under the name of Torguts.

All these different races were kept in order by a military force of Manchus and Chinese, with a Jan-jun, or governor-general, living in Ili Kulja, while the Amban of Eastern Turkestan, residing at Kashgar, and that of Tarbagatai, resident at Chuguchak, were subject to him.

This state of things continued, with occasional disturbances, and especially risings of the Mohammedan khojas, in Kashgar, till the grand Mohammedan upheaval in China, when for a time the Imperial authority was swept away, and a Mohammedan kingdom was established in Turkestan by Yakub Beg.

This is not the place to give a detailed history of the rise and consolidation of Yakub Beg's power, and I would refer any who are interested in the subject to Dr. Bellew's work Kashmir and Kashgar—for a full description of the country under the Ameer's rule. So long as he lived it appeared that the prestige of his successes, and the vigour of his administration would render the task of Tso Tsung Tang, the Chinese general appointed by the Court of Peking to reorganize the country, a very hopeless business. But what was denied to the half-starved, ill-disciplined forces under his command, was accomplished by the hand of an assassin. Those who were in London last year may have observed the fine manly figure of an Oriental prince, whose countenance and demeanour won for its possessor golden opinions in English society. Syud Yakub Khan, nephew and chief adviser of the late Ameer, had come to England not merely to repeat the sentiment of friendship which his uncle felt and heartily expressed towards her Majesty the Queen, but he had another object in view, viz. to bring about, if possible, an amicable understanding between the Chinese Government and his master, by which Yakub Khan might retain possession of the country he had won by his sword, at the same time, yielding allegiance to the Chinese, as sovereigns of the land. But whilst negotiations were progressing between the two parties news came of the assassination of the Ameer, and of consequent disturbances in the State of Kashgar.

It followed as a matter of course, that the dissensions and internecine feuds which at once sprang up, afforded a splendid opportunity for the advance of Tso and his Chinese army, and he soon found himself courted and welcomed by the inhabitants of Aksu and other cities who were anxious to throw off the Mohammedan yoke. Even Niaz Beg, the Mohammedan ruler, under the Ameer of Khoten, sent messengers to invite the advent of the Chinese, and went into open rebellion against the Ameer's son Beg Kuli Beg, who was wounded in a fight with his rebellious lieutenant. The Governor of Kashgar, Alish Khan Dadkhah, for a time restored the fortunes of the family, by defeating the force of the late Ameer's murderer, Hakim Khan Tura. But Beg Kuli Beg soon afterwards stained his hands by the murder of his young brother, Hak Kuli Beg, and the drama closed on the 5th December, when Beg Kuli Beg and his followers fled from the city of Kashgar, and took refuge in Russian territory. It is worthy of note, that some English merchants who remained in Yarkand after the Ameer's death, and during the first few months of the subsequent disturbance, were in no way molested, but returned to India in perfect safety at the end of the year.

It is curious and at the same time interesting to go back just ten years, and read once more by the light of recent events the brilliant article in

the *Edinburgh Review* on Western China. Had
the talented writer of that article lived, how
vividly would he have depicted the rise and fall
of the Mohammedan power in Eastern Turkestan.
It would be waste of time and a vain effort on
my part to attempt to recapitulate here the tale
which has been so admirably told by Mr. Wyllie,
of the progress of the Mohammedan insurrection
against the yoke of the Chinese, which culminated
in the establishment of Yakub Beg's complete
ascendancy over the whole of what was called
Altyshahr. But I cannot refrain from doing
more justice to the memory of the late Ameer
Yakub Beg than the able reviewer was disposed
to award him. The bare idea of despatching an
embassy to Central Asia aroused in the mind of
the Reviewer feelings of the bitterest hostility,
and called forth what he himself admits was
strong language regarding the ignorant temerity
of officers who would place their lives in the
hands of the bloodthirsty and perfidious bar-
barians of Central Asia. But very soon afterwards the triumphant return of Messrs. Shaw
and Hayward from a lengthened sojourn in Kashgar, when they were the honoured guests of the
Kushbegee Yakub Beg, taught us to moderate
the fears which had been excited by the Reviewer;
and the subsequent intercourse which Europeans,
both commercial agents and officials, have main-
tained with that country, so long as Yakub Beg's

rule lasted, has completely falsified Mr. Wyllie's prediction. But on another point Mr. Wyllie's hopes proved to be well founded. The Kush-begee or Ameer, not being a mere soldier of fortune, but something of a statesman also, the first use he made of the consolidation of his conquests was to resuscitate the trade which recent wars and tumults had all but extinguished in Eastern Turkestan. Opinions are very much divided as to the extent of expansion of which this trade is capable; but sufficient improvement has taken place within this decade, to make it desirable to continue our fostering care. In the days of the Chinese supremacy, the commerce with Yarkand was next to nothing, and was looked upon by the Chinese as contraband. Now that they have regained possession of the country, it is to be hoped that they will profit by the lesson which has been taught them in another province of China, where rebellion was put down, but where they have lately been compelled to admit Western civilization through the door which the Moham-medans of Yunnan opened during the short period of their emancipation.

It would be for the interest of the Chinese quite as much as for the benefit of British trade that a British consul should be established at Yarkand or Kashgar, to regulate trade and to maintain friendly relations. In former days the chief business done by our traders with Eastern

Turkestan was in opium, which they smuggled across the Karakorum and sold for enormous profit in Yarkand and Khoten. This pernicious trade ceased entirely when the Chinese disappeared, and its place was taken by a much more healthy commerce in tea and English piece-goods.

Are we now to revert to the old state of things, shut up the export of Manchester goods and take to smuggling opium? I trust not, indeed. The subject is one well worthy the attention of the Indian authorities.

Colonel Prejevalsky complains of the very strict surveillance to which he was subjected during his stay in the dominions of Yakub Beg. Doubtless it was very annoying, and it might be even disappointing to find after all the friendly intercourse with both Russians and English, and the exchange of treaties of friendship, that freedom of action was still denied to European travellers.

But we must not judge Asiatics as we would judge European princes. There was ancient custom to guide him, and if the Ameer knew anything of history, he might fairly plead excuse for his alarm at a too unrestricted influx of foreigners. The ancient custom to which I have referred was to keep all foreign travellers more or less in confinement, and always under the strictest surveillance. Mr. Shaw, in the very interesting account of his adventurous journey to the court of the Atalik Ghazee, tells us how he was treated on the road, with the utmost kindness and hospitality, but always as a kind of state prisoner. During the whole of his stay in Yarkand and Kashgar he was not once allowed to go outside the quarters assigned to him, except on a visit to the authorities. Force was never employed, but, on the contrary, he was continually deceived by an apparent anxiety to meet his wishes for an enlargement of his confinement; but somehow or other, in a most clever manner, without giving him ground for actual quarrel, some untoward circumstance arose to prevent his breaking through his restraint. Hayward, who was more impetuous, broke through the cordon of guardians, and caused considerable trouble and apprehension in the mind of his fellow-traveller, lest by so doing he had jeopardized their lives.

When Lord Mayo despatched the first mission to Yarkand in 1870, I endeavoured to stipulate with Mirza Shadee, the Atalik's envoy, that freedom of movement should be granted to us. This he promised, though he explained that it was the unvarying custom in Central Asia to keep all envoys in confinement at the court to which they were accredited, and even to lead them blindfold through the streets. On arrival in Yarkand territory we found Mirza Shadee somewhat slow to keep his promise, and Dr. Henderson relates the state of excitement into which the envoy was thrown, on discovering that he had fallen behind our party, in order to shoot some specimens of birds. And when we reached Yarkand, Mirza Shadee considered himself altogether absolved from his promise, and an attempt, which was successfully but with great difficulty resisted, was made to subject us to the same confinement as Messrs. Shaw and Hayward had undergone.

When the second mission was sent in 1873 all doubt on this point was cleared up at the outset, and within certain limits no restraint whatever was put upon our movements. At first spies in the shape of escorts were always attached to us. But even this precaution was in time dropped, and we were allowed to come and go just as we liked.   But all this was within certain limits. Distant expeditions to Aksu, Korla, and Lake Lob, though often promised, were finally forbidden; a visit to Khoten, which was at first suggested to me, and subsequently talked of as a matter of course, was at last peremptorily prohibited, and it was only after some diplomatic fencing that I was able to despatch a party across the Pamir. All this conduct was very disappointing, quite as much so to us as it was to Colonel Prejevalsky; but on looking back on the whole circumstances, I cannot altogether blame the Ameer for acting according to his light.   In addition to the ancient custom pleaded by Mirza Shader, there was another very potent reason for shyness on the part of our Asiatic

chief to receive strangers unrestrained. From
the earliest times the gold-fields of Khoten have
been known to exist, though as yet they have
never been visited by any European. The
scientific researches of Dr. Stoliczka revealed to
the Ameer of Kashgar the existence of rich mines
of copper, lead, coal, and other hidden wealth,
all which treasures the Ameer showed his wisdom
in wishing to keep for his own use; and he could
not be altogether unacquainted with the fact that
foreigners who travel in Asia to explore too often
stay to annex.

And as regards Colonel Prejevalsky and the
advent of Russians in Eastern Turkestan, Yakub
Beg was doubtless aware of ancient traditions,
as are recorded by Mons. Gregorieff, and more
lately by Howorth in his History of the Mongols.

Like most other countries, Russia has had its
romantic El Dorado, a land outside its borders,
where it has fancied wealth and ease might be
bought easily by washing gold out of a river, and
which led to some adventurous journeys. This
El Dorado was the country of little Bukharia,
and especially the neighbourhood of Yarkand
(and Khoten) reported to be rich in gold deposits.

In 1714, Prince Gagarin, Governor of Siberia,
presented a report, in which he suggested that it
would be possible to appropriate this country,
and he suggested that a series of forts should be
pushed along from the Irtish as far as Yarkand,

to form a protection through the Kalmuk territory. With the note he sent specimens of the
gold dust which had been taken to Tobolsk for
sale. In consequence of this, Ivan Bukholz was
ordered by the Emperor to repair to Siberia, and
having collected a force of 2000 or 3000 men to
proceed to build a fort near the Lake Yamish,
and then, if possible, to make his way to Yarkand.
Bukholz so far carried out his orders that he
built a fortress on the Yamish which was viewed
by the Kalmuks as an invasion of their territory,
which they for the time successfully repelled; but
as we know, the power of Russia gradually spread
with irresistible force. In 1718 the fort of Semipalatinsk was built, and by A.D. 1720 the Russians
had reached Lake Zaisan. This, says Mr. Howorth,
was apparently the last attempt made by the Russians to reach the gold country of Yarkand. But
this is not so. Gradually but persistently they
have advanced towards the golden land. They
occupy Kulja, and have brought their boundary
line to the Robat Pass and Chadir Kul, within
110 miles of Kashgar, and this journey of
Colonel Prejevalsky had for its object the
thorough exploration of the route by the gold-
fields of Khoten to Tibet, and it is not surprising that the Ameer should watch his proceedings with more than ordinary interest.

During the stay of the English Mission in Kashgar in 1873-74, good opportunity was afforded for

obtaining information regarding the very interesting countries under the sway of the late Ameer Yakub Beg. A few extracts from the official report which has not yet been more than sparsely published may be useful in throwing additional light on the particular region traversed by Col. Prejevalsky.

The chief cities on the southern slopes of the Tian Shan range are Aksu, Kucha, Korla, Karashahr, and will be noticed in order. Aksu is a very ancient city, and was formerly called Arpadil or Ardabil. It is situated at the base of the Tian Shan range at the southern entrance to the Muzart or Glacier Pass. It covers two ridges of gravel heights on the left bank of the Aksu river, where it is joined by the Ush or Kokshal river, and has a citadel on each ridge. This city was destroyed by earthquake in A.D. 1716. The climate is described as very salubrious, though the winters are extremely rigorous. The citizens are peaceable and industrious. They are more purely Turk in their physiognomy than the citizens of Kashgar or Yarkand, and are supposed to be the people of Artush, north of Kashgar, the purest representatives of the ancient Uighur conquerors.

Aksu is celebrated for its manufactures of saddlery and harness, its pottery, and rude hide jars. Its tobacco is considered the best that is produced in the country. The mineral resources of the country are considerable, and mines of lead,

copper, and sulphur have been systematically
worked, whilst coal is used in the city as fuel.
The lead-mines are in Tajik Tagh, about twenty-five
miles off the city, and those of copper are at On-
bash, on the Muzart river. In the vicinity of the city
are hot sulphur springs, which are resorted to by
the inhabitants for medicinal purposes. There is
also an active volcano, from the base of which are
collected alum, sal-ammoniac, and blue vitriol or
sulphate of copper. The asbestos mentioned by
Marco Polo as an utilized product of this region is
not even so known in this country.

The Muzart or Mussart Pass connects this division with Ili or Kulja. The road by this pass
crosses an enormous glacier, which is interrupted
by vast fissures and massive banks, and unless
constantly kept open by gangs of labourers,
becomes speedily impassable.

Kucha is a small state situated at the foot of the
mountain, in continuation eastward from Aksu.
In ancient times it was an important little princi-
pality, and a flourishing seat of Buddhism. On a
hill to the north of the city are the ruins of an
ancient temple and monastery. They are described
as of considerable extent, and very substantially
built of stone on the ledges and rocks of a precipitous hill.

Fragments of sculptures are found among the
débris, and in some galleries sunk in the rock
there are paintings of men and animals on the

walls as fresh and bright in colour as if they were new. Precious stones, gems, and trinkets are occasionally found in the rubbish of the crumbled walls, and marvellous tales are told of the lustre and size of some that have been picked up here by wandering shepherds. A large figure is said to exist here, carved on the face of a rock overlooking the road to Korla. It is described as having the tongue lolled out, and right shoulder depressed with extended arm, as in the fashion of the Kalmuk salutation. It acknowledges the salutes of passers by a return wag of the tongue and wink of the eye, and has been often seen to smile, by credulous Kalmuks at least.

In the mountains to the north is a volcano, and from its base a river called Zamcha issues. On its banks are dry alum and a salt of zinc called Zamch, which is used as a mordant with alum in dyeing. The rocks at the foot of the hill are hot to the touch, but the water of the river is cold. Loud rumblings and explosions are constantly heard in the interior of the mountain, which is very high, and whose top is always covered with snow. It is called Khan Khura Tagh, and forms the boundary between Yulduz of the Kalmuk and Junghar of the Kirghiz and Kassak, who are also called Juttah (or Jété) Moghols.

Khan Khura Tagh is the western boundary of the Yulduz territory, and has a live volcano. This Yulduz Valley is celebrated throughout the region of Central Asia for its beauty, its springs, meadows, and fine breezes. The farmsteads are described as models of neatness and thrift, and the orchards produce the finest apples and pears, and pomegranates in the country. The pears are of a peculiar excellence, of light colour, soft granular structure, and very juicy. The apples are of a peculiar kind called Muzalma, or Ice apple, their skin being transparent, and the substance the same as if iced.

This valley was the favourite camping-ground of Timour after his campaign of extermination against the Juts.

A native of these parts, speaking in raptures of the delights of this valley, said, "Just as you think Kashmir superior to all the rest of the world, so is Yulduz superior to Kashmir."

Korla is the next division, at the foot of the Khan Khura range, and the town of that name is the one where Colonel Prejevalsky first came in contact with Yakub Beg's officials.

The next division eastward, is Karashahr, which occupies a valley between the Uighur Bulak to the north (a continuation eastward of the Alatagh or Tengri Ula range), and the Kurugh Tagh range of sandhills to the south. These coalesce towards the east and close the valley in that direction at Gumish Akma, about ninety miles from the city, but towards the west the valley is open, and gives passage to the Kaidu river, which, on crossing from the Yulduz valley, spreads over the southern portion of this basin, and forms the Baghrash Kol or lake, which is described as a long sheet of water, five days' journey in length, and covered with floating islands of tall reeds, amidst which the river flows in the western end of the lake only. It is separated from the Lob district to the south by the Kurugh Tagh, a wide range of sandy and gravelly ridges, amongst the hollows of which the wild horse and wild camel breed. There is a road between the lake and this range, seven days' journey from Korla to Ush Aktal, and there is another along its southern side, between it and Lob, seven days' journey from Kara Koshun to Turfan. The city of Karashahr stands near the left bank of the river, to the north of the lake. Fifty miles north-east of this city is Ush Aktal, and twenty miles beyond it, and about the same distance from Gumish Akma, where the road enters the hills, there are the ruins of an ancient city, called Kara Kizil, which are supposed to be the remains of the ancient Jalish or Chalish.

Colonel Prejevalsky's actual observations at Lake Lob are exceedingly interesting, as they corroborate much that appeared doubtful in the accounts received from former travellers. As Marco Polo in former times, and Colonel Yule at the present day, are the great authorities on all matters connected with the geography, and to a

great extent of the history of Central Asia, I
will take these authorities first.

Marco Polo mentions a city called Lob or Lop,
five days' journey from Charchan, at the entrance of
the Great Desert, the inhabitants of the city being
Mohammedans. Such persons as purpose to
cross the Desert, take a week's rest in the town to
refresh themselves and their cattle, and then they
make ready for the journey, taking with them a
month's supply for man and beast. On quitting the
city they enter the desert.

Colonel Yule, in his copious notes, endeavoured
to fix the longitude of Lop, placing it three degrees
more to the westward than it is put in our maps,
putting it, in fact, in 88° E. of Greenwich. Colonel
Prejevalsky has now scientifically fixed its position.
Regarding the ancient cities buried in the sand,
which have been said to exist in these regions, we
now have Colonel Prejevalsky's testimony, but it
is unfortunate that he was unable to make excava-
tions or any extended explorations, or he might
have enabled us to award the exact value to a curious
description of the ruins of one city given by a
Kirghiz traveller, and contained in the report of
the Yarkand Mission. He says (see page 46) :—

"They are on the desert to the east of the
Katak ruins, and three days' journey from Lob, in
a south-west direction along the course of the
Khoten river. The walls are seen rising above
the reeds in which the city is concealed. I have

not been inside the city, but I have seen its walls distinctly from the sandy ridge in the vicinity. I was afraid to go amongst the ruins because of the bogs around and the venomous insects and snakes in the reeds. I was camped about them for several days with a party of Lob shepherds who were here pasturing their cattle. Besides it is a notorious fact that people who do go amongst the ruins almost always die, because they cannot resist the temptation to steal the gold and precious things stored there."

Another statement of his is as follows (page 30) :—

"Nobody can go more than three or four days' journey to the east of the lake, owing to the depth of the soft powdery saline soil, on which neither man nor beast can find footing. From the lake a river goes out to the south-east, across an immense desert of this salt and sand. At fifteen days' or twenty days' journey it passes under a mountain, and reappears on the other side, in China. In olden times a young man of Lob went in his boat to explore the river beyond the lake. After going down the stream for seven days he saw a mountain ahead, and on going closer he found the river entered a frightful black and deep chasm in the rocks. He tried to stop his boat, but the swiftness of the current carried it into the chasm. At its farther end he saw a small black hole inside the mountain, and had only time to lie down in the bottom of the boat, when it was drawn into the dark passage. The top of the boat scraped the roof of the channel, and bits of stone continually fell upon him. After a long time he emerged from the darkness into light, and found the bottom of his boat strewed with nuggets of gold. He went down the river for some days, and finally found himself in Peking."

In the mythical geography of the Chinese, less exaggerated than that of the Hindoos nevertheless, the Hoang Ho is made to rise in the eastern slopes of the Bolor. By the river Tarim, and by a subterranean passage, they placed it in communication with Lake Lob, which they thought was a part of a vast dried-up sea, and which, according to M. Lassen, has given the Hindoos the first notion of a northern sea.

This story would appear to be the popular mode of accounting for the belief that the river Tarim, flowing through Lake Lob, and being apparently lost in the Great Desert, in reality reappears in China as the great Hoang Ho, or Yellow River.

The idea that the waters of the Tarim, flowing through Lake Lob, communicate with a large Chinese river, which empties itself into the sea, seems to have prevailed from early times until now. In the Tarikhi Rashidi, of Mirza Haidar, Lake Lob is mentioned as covering an area four months' journey in circuit, and as giving exit to the great Kara Moran river of China. Since that time there has been a gradual desiccation, and a recent traveller, a native of those regions, thus describes the tract:—"Lob is a succession of lakes along the Tarim river. Each lake gives off five or six streams, which spread over the plain and reunite lower down to form the next lake, and so on for a journey of thirty days by the road. Beyond this is the great desert, of which nobody knows anything."

Humboldt in his "Asie Centrale" makes the following remarks:—

"It is one of the chief geographical features of the country that to the east of the great river of Khoten (Khoten-daria or Youroung-Kach-gol), which, after a course of three hundred miles from south to north, flows into the water system of the Tarim and of Lake Lob, all the streams of the two slopes of the Kuen-lun are lost in the small lakes of the steppes.

"In this central region, between the 80° and 90° longitude, the upheaval of the Gobi makes itself felt in the course of the streams, an upheaval which causes an entirely independent direction of profile (*accident du relief*) to that of the sand-ripples which cover it, far more ancient than these, and probably connected with the first appearance of the continent above the waters.

"The intersection offered by the Gobi, the Kuen-lun, and the Tian-Shan, must not therefore be confounded with the interlacement of

two ranges; as for instance, of the Bolor or of the
meridian chains to the east of the river Tzang-bo-
schou with the Hindoo Khoosh and the Himalayas. The phenomenon which we describe is of
quite a different nature. The upheaval of the
Plateau of Gobi, stretching from S.W. to N.E.,
and, according to the most exact barometrical
measurements taken in the 43° and 48° of latitude,
about four thousand feet mean height, is perhaps
of the same age as the great Aralo-Caspian
depression."

The account of the Lob district, given in the
Report of the Yarkand Mission, may be advan-
tageously compared with Colonel Prejevalsky's
personal observations.

Lob is the name of a district on the banks of
the Tarim river, which is formed by the union of
all the rivers from Yulduz, of Ili, round by
the western circuit of Kashgar to Khoten and
Charchan.

Lob was only peopled 160 years ago by emi-
grant families of the Kara Kalmuk, Koshot, Tor-
gute, &c., to the number of 1000 houses. They are
now all professedly Mussulmans, and have Mulla
and Imam priests amongst them, but they do not
know much about Islam. There were people in
Lob before these Kalmuk emigrants came, but
nothing is known regarding them. They are
called " wild " people, because they delight to live
with the wild beasts and their cattle in the thickets

and brakes about the marshes. They are small, black men, with long matted hair, and shun the society of other men. Whenever they see any strangers, they run away and hide in the thickets and reeds. Nobody knows whence they came, or where they live, and nobody understands their language. They are very timid, but, though only armed with bow and arrow, and long pike, are brave hunters. They keep cattle, and have no cultivation. They wear clothes of a coarse strong material called luf, the fibre of a plant which has a flower and a pod like the wild liquorice. It protects the wearer from the attacks of gnats and mosquitoes, which never alight on this cloth.

The population of the Lob settlement is reckoned at 1000 houses. There are no permanent houses, but the inhabitants live in reed huts, or else in boats. There is no cultivation, and the people live on fish, and the produce of their flocks and of the chase. They govern themselves according to their own customs, and are little interfered with by the authorities. At all events, during the Ameer's rule it would appear that there was little hope of getting any revenue out of them. Some of their customs, as told to Dr. Bellew, are peculiar. They always swear upon the gun, and if any one wishes to free himself from an accusation, he appeals to the accuser to produce his gun, and kissing the muzzle, places it against his breast, and bids him fire. This throws the responsibility on the accuser, who on this proof of innocence retracts his calumny.

Another somewhat peculiar custom is thus related by Dr. Bellew. During the spring and summer seasons the young people are in the habit of racing along the river. A party of six or eight maids form up on the river, each in her own skiff, and a party of as many youths form up on the bank, each on his own horse. At an agreed signal they all start off to an appointed goal, the maids paddling down the stream, and the youths galloping along the bank. If the maids win, they select a partner for the night from amongst the youths, each in the order of her arrival at the winning-post. Similarly if the youths win, they choose their companion from the maids in turn. The contract only lasts for that night, and the couplings vary with the chances of each successive race, though often the same partners meet. If a girl becomes pregnant she points out the author, and he marries her.

T. DOUGLAS FORSYTH.

Note.—Many of these remarks have been taken from the official narrative of the Mission to Kashgar in 1873, which has not been published to the world.—T. D. F.

TRAVELS TO LOB-NOR.

CHAPTER I.

ANOTHER successful step in the exploration of Inner
Asia—the basin of Lob-nor, so long and so
obstinate a *terra incognita*—has at length been
revealed to science.

As originally contemplated, the starting-point
of my expedition was the town of Kulja.[1] Here
I arrived at the end of July, 1876, with my two

[1] [There were two towns of this name, about twenty-five miles
apart. The one mentioned in the text is the old Tartar town,
now the head-quarters of the Russian administration of the
province of Ili; the other, New or Manchu Kulja, was a
flourishing Chinese city of about 75,000 inhabitants until the
late Mohammedan rising, when it was taken by the rebels, the
whole population put to the sword, and the city reduced to ashes.
See Schuyler's *Turkistan*, ii. 162 *et seqq.*—M.]

companions, Lieut. Povalo-Schweikofsky, and a
volunteer of the name of Eklon. Adequately
supplied this time with funds, I was able to buy
in St. Petersburg and Moscow all the requisite
stores for so long a journey, and these, together
with guns and ammunition (the latter supplied by
Government), weighed about two tons. This
weight I had to transport from Perm to Kulja on
five postal troikas which took me more than a
month, delayed by the abominable state of the
roads in crossing the Ural.

At Semipalatinsk we were joined by the companions of my last expedition to Mongolia—the
Trans-Baikalian Cossacks, Chebayeff and Irin-
chinoff, who declared their readiness to share with
me once again the hardships and privations of a
new journey. One other Cossack was also sent
from Trans-Baikalia to act as interpreter of the
Mongol language, and I took three others at
Vernoye from the Semiretchinsk force. Lastly,
at Kulja itself I hired a Kirghiz Christian convert,
who spoke the Sart language. In this way the
personnel of my expedition was formed, but un-
fortunately I was not nearly so successful in the
choice of my companions as I had been on the
last occasion.

Nearly three weeks were occupied at Kulja in
the final formation and equipment of our caravan,
consisting of twenty-four camels and four riding-
horses. The latter were bestridden by myself, my

companions, and one of the Cossacks.   We were all admirably armed; besides fowling-pieces each carried a Berdan rifle swung over the shoulder, and a brace of pistols in our holsters.

Our original plan was to proceed to Lob-nor, explore as much of this lake and its environs as possible, and then return to Kulja, leave our collections here, and taking our remaining supplies, start for Tibet.

On the morning of the 12th of August we took our departure from Kulja, accompanied by the good wishes of our countrymen resident at that town.

Our road lay at first up and almost alongside the bank of the Ili, whose valley is here thickly settled by Taranchis.[2] Clean, pretty villages with gardens, shaded by lofty silver poplars, follow each other in quick succession.   In the intervals are corn-fields irrigated by numerous watercourses, whilst on the meadows along the river's bank large herds of sheep, oxen, and horses are grazing.[3] The population is everywhere apparently prosperous; the Mohammedan rising never having

[2] [These were agricultural colonists from Eastern Turkistan, of whom Sir D. Forsyth has spoken in his introductory remarks. According to M. Radloff, quoted by Schuyler, their language is more specifically Turkish than that of any book published at Constantinople.—*Turkistan*, ii. 169 *seq.*—M.]

[3] [Schuyler, who visited the Ili valley in 1873, thought it the richest part of Russia's recent acquisitions in Asia.—ii. 198. —M.]

D

desolated this part of the valley. The districts
which were laid waste lie below Kulja, following
the Ili. Here, too, agriculture once flourished,
but since the extermination of the Chinese inhabitants by the Taranchis and Dungans, the villages
are mostly destroyed, and even such towns as Old
Kulja, Bayandai, Chimpanzi, and others are in
ruins, the fields deserted and choked with weeds.
After crossing to the left bank of the Ili, near the
mouth of the Kash (fifty versts beyond Kulja), we
continued as before to ascend its valley, in this
part twenty versts wide, and having the appearance of a steppe plain with a clayey and slightly
saline soil, producing *Ceratocarpus*, dwarf wormwood, and *Lasiogrostis ;* in the more fertile part
astragalus, a few kinds of herbs or plants of the
order *compositæ*, and small gnarled bushes ; whilst
the river bank is fringed with thick cane-brake.

The width of the Ili near the mouth of the Kash
is about 500 feet, with a very rapid stream.   Taranchi villages continue for twelve versts further
up the right bank from the confluence of the Kash
—the left bank has no settled population.   Here
only occasional fields temporarily tilled by the
Kalmuks may be seen, and these only nearer the
river Tekes.   The last-named stream flows from
the Mussart, and unites with the Kunges to form
the Ili, which empties its muddy waters into Lake
Balkash.   [See supplementary note.]

The Tekes, here 350 feet wide, with a terribly

swift stream, is crossed in small, rotten ferry-boats. On these our baggage was taken across; the horses and camels were fastened behind the boat, and were made to swim to the opposite bank. This swim proved very injurious to the camels, and three soon afterwards died from the effects of it. Beyond the Tekes our road lay continually in the same easterly direction by the valley of the Lower Kunges,[4] which is hardly distinguishable from that of the Upper Ili, excepting that feather-grass is more abundant. The hills, bordering the valley as before, are covered with grass, rounded in out-line, and totally bare of trees as far as the river Tsanma. Here the traveller sees the last of the fields and encampments of the Turgutes;[5] beyond his point, as far as the Kara-shahr valley, no in-habitants are to be met with. The flora of the plain we had hitherto traversed from Kulja was very scanty; and the fauna equally deficient. The season too (latter half of August) was most un-favourable for ornithological researches and pre-paring skins, many of the birds being in the moulting stage. But snakes and lizards were

[4] [Colonel Yule informs me that the route followed by Colonel Prejevalsky seems to be the same as that of Shah Rukh's em-bassy to China in 1420, which went by the Kunges and Yulduz to Turfan.—M.]

[5] [The Turgutes or Torgutes, as already mentioned (*vide supra*, introductory remarks), are the Kalmuks of the present day, of whom remnants still exist on the Lower Volga.—See Wallace's *Russia*, ii. 52; and see also pp. 169—186 of this work.—M.]

very abundant, and we collected a good number
of these reptiles. Of fish we only caught four
kinds; *Dyptichus*, *Schizothorax*, perch, and gudgeon.
According to the Cossacks, who are great fishermen, there are no others in the Ili.

As the elevation of the country rises beyond
the Tsanma,[6] the valley of the Kunges changes its
character, and becomes narrower and more fertile.
Instead of the clumps of vegetation we had
hitherto seen, excellent and varied herbage clothed
the undulating plain, growing higher and thicker
every ten versts or so as we advanced; the outline
of the marginal hills became sterner, and spruce
firs began to show themselves, their lower belt
marking the limit of the summer rains.

Rain, however, does fall, although perhaps
less abundantly, in the steppe zone, where the
elevation is 4000 feet, or even somewhat less. At
this point larch woods begin growing on the banks
of the Kunges itself, interspersed with tall poplars
(some 80ft. high, with stems 3ft. and 5ft. thick)
and apple-trees; birch and apricot are more rare.
The thick underwood is composed of hawthorn,
cherry, woodbine, guelder rose, and briar. The
islands in the river are thickly overgrown with
tall *salix* or willow, round whose stems the wild

---

[6] Kulja is about 2000 feet above sea-level. It should be
noticed that although the heights have all been measured
barometrically, the results obtained have as yet only been
worked out approximately.

hop is often twined, and tamarisk appears on the
sandy and stony spots.   The woodland meadows
and slopes of the neighbouring hills are everywhere clothed with the thickest grass, interwoven
with convolvulus and dodder, often 7ft. high and
almost impassable in summer.   But at the season
we arrived on the Kunges (early in September)
the grass was withering and dying down, and the
trees and bushes had donned their autumnal
attire.

After the monotony of steppe scenery, the
wooded islands and banks of the Kunges produced
an agreeable impression, and yielding to its
influence we determined on making some stay in
this highly-favoured little corner of the Tian
Shan.   Here, too, we could reckon on a rich,
scientific harvest.   Moreover, two of our Cossacks
had proved unserviceable for travel, and we were
obliged to send them back to Kulja and exchange
them for two soldiers, whose arrival could not be
expected for ten days.[1]

We selected for our camping-ground in the
forests of Kunges the very spot occupied for some
months in 1874 by one of our sotnias of Cossacks.
Here the shed they had erected, their kitchen and
bath-house were still standing; we too enjoyed a
good and final wash in this bath-house before
starting for the Tian Shan.

---

[1] Our Kirghiz interpreter also proved worthless, and he had
also to return to Kulja and be replaced by a new one.

One remarkable characteristic of the Kunges forests, and probably of other wooded glens on the northern slope of the Tian Shan is the great abundance of apple and apricot-trees [8] producing excellent fruit. The apricots, or as they are here called, *uriuk*, ripen in July; the apples by the end of August. The latter are about the size of a hen's egg, pale yellow in colour, and with an agreeable bitter-sweet flavour. We were just in time for the apple harvest on the Kunges; the trees were laden with the fruit, quantities of which strewed the ground, where they decay without benefiting any one, or are devoured by wild boar, bears, deer, and goats, which at this season of the year descend in numbers from the adjacent hills. Wild boar and bears are particularly addicted to apples, and the latter are known to indulge to excess in their favourite dainty.

Our sport with the larger game was tolerably successful, and we secured some fine specimens for our collection; amongst these an old dark-brown bear of a species peculiar to the Tian Shan, and distinguishable from the common bruin by the long white claws on the fore-feet— a peculiarity which induced Sévertseff to name it *Ursus leuconyx*.[9]

---

[8] [Compare Aristof's description of the Kunges valley, quoted by Schuyler.—*Turkistan*, ii. 199 *seqq.*—M.]

[9] Sévertseff identifies his *Ursus leuconyx* with *U. isabel-*

Besides four-footed beasts, the forests on the
Kunges contained many a migratory woodcock
and thrush (*Turdus atrigularis, T. viscivorus*), and
numbers of corncrakes and landrail on the
meadow-land.   Many of the nesting birds had
departed for the south; of non-migratory we only
found an occasional pheasant (*Ph. mongolicus*),
blue tits (*Cyanistes cyanus*), woodpeckers, and
a few others.   The autumnal flight is generally
very deficient in this part of the Tian Shan, even
in small birds.

A range of no great elevation, crossed by a pass
6000 feet high, separates the Kunges from the broad
valley of the Tsanma, the river we had already
crossed near its mouth.   Although not more than
eight versts apart, the difference in the height of
the respective valleys of the Kunges and Tsanma
is nearly 2000 feet.   From the pass itself may be
seen, as from an opera-box, on one side the comparatively low and deeply indented Kunges valley, on
the other the elevated basin of the river Tsanma.

The latter is about four versts wide, and
thickly clothed with high grass.   Along the
upper course of the river, commencing at an

linus Horsf. from the Himalayas.   But in my opinion they are
two distinct species.   The Himalayan bear is also met with in
the Tian Shan, where it is only known to inhabit the elevated
plateaux devoid of trees and the Alpine region, never entering
the forest zone.   Besides, *U. isabellinus* is of a tawny colour;
U. leuconyx, on the other hand, is dark brown, like the European
U. arctos.

elevation of 6000 feet, are forests, whose prevailing trees are the Tian Shan spruce [1] (*Picea Schrenki-ana*), the mountain ash now taking the place of the apple or apricot-trees. Spruce firs are also scattered in clumps over the neighbouring mountains, growing as high as 8000 feet and even upwards above the sea level.

The approach of autumn now began to be felt in the mountains. Not very long ago we had been oppressed by the heat on the Ili plain; now, on the contrary, every morning brought light frosts, snow lay on all the higher mountains, the trees and bushes were shorn of half their foliage. But the weather continued bright and clear, and during the day it would even be hot at times.

After having ascended the Kunges, and afterwards the Tsanma to its source, we moved towards the foot of the Narat range, which, with its western prolongations,[2] forms the northern buttress of an extensive and lofty plateau situated in the very heart of the Tian Shan, and known by the name of Yulduz.

---

[1] This tree attains a height of seventy to eighty feet, with a thickness of stem two, three, and often four feet in diameter. It grows very much in the sugar-loaf shape, its thick branches hardly projecting from the general mass, so that the whole tree has the appearance of having been cropped by a barber.

[2] The western prolongations of the Narat range, taking them in their order, are the *Dagat*, *Kara-nor*, *Koko-sung*, and *Djamba-daban* ranges; the three last-named are said to be capped with eternal snows.

Before describing Yulduz, let us say a few words about the Narat. This range though nowhere reaching the limit of the perpetual snow-line, presents nevertheless a wild and alpine character. Its solitary peaks with their steep slopes, particularly near the axis of the range, are scored with bare precipitous cliffs forming narrow gloomy chasms. Below these again are the alpine meadows, and lower still on the northern side clumps of spruce fir; the southern slopes of the Narat are treeless.

We crossed this range at its eastern extremity, where the ascent is not particularly steep, though difficult for camels; on the Yulduz side the descent is very gradual. Snow lay in small quantities on the northern slopes during our march, i. e. in the middle of September, whereas on its south side the Narat was completely free of snow. The pass is 9800 feet above sea-level. Near the summit we killed a small boar, preserving its skin for our collection, and its meat for our provision-store.

Descending the Narat, we entered Yulduz. This name signifies " star," and was perhaps bestowed on the country owing to its elevated position among the mountains, or from the circumstance of its being the promised land of cattle.[1] The

---

[1] [According to Bellew, Yulduz was the son of Manglai, the son of Timurtash—" Ironstone "—a descendant of Kaian. He raised the Mongol name to the highest fame, and was the ancestor of all the Mongol Khans. (Report of a mission to

pasturage is excellent in every part, and it enjoys
in summer an immunity from flies and mosquitoes,
"an admirable, cool, and productive country,
fit for gentlemen and cattle to inhabit," as the
Torgutes described it to us. It forms an extensive
depression continuing for some hundreds of versts
from east to west. In all probability it was at
some remote geological epoch the bed of an inland
sea, as its alluvial clay soil tends to prove. Yulduz
consists of two parts : Greater Yulduz occupying
the more extensive westerly half of the whole
depression, and Lesser Yulduz the smaller eastern
part. Both of these have the same general features, the difference between them consisting only
in their size. Lesser Yulduz, along the whole of
which we passed, has the appearance of a steppe-
plain extending lengthways for 135 versts, and
widening in the centre to thirty versts.

Near the marginal mountains this plain is
hillocky, and covered with luxuriant herbage.
Here, too, chiefly in its eastern part grow low,
stunted bushes of camel thorn, willow, and *Potentilla;* of trees there are none in Yulduz.

The elevation of Lesser Yulduz is from 7000 to
8000 feet above sea-level.[4] The marginal ranges
on the north and south are wild, rocky, and of

Yarkand in 1873, p. 136.)   May not the country have derived
its name from him, for it was all under Mongol dominion ?—M.].

[4] The lowest parts are on the lower course of the Baga
Yulduz-gol ; on its upper stream and nearer the marginal
mountains the country is higher.

great elevation, not only above the level of the sea, but also above that of the adjacent plain; the southern range, dividing Lesser from Greater Yulduz, rises in several places above the limit of perpetual snow.[5] Exactly in the centre of Lesser Yulduz, and throughout its entire length, flows the Baga Yulduz-gol, uniting with the Kaidu-gol after the latter has drained Greater Yulduz, and finally emptying into Lake Bagarash.

We forded the Baga Yulduz-gol, but in spring and summer the water is too high to allow of the fords being practicable. Fish are plentiful, both in the Baga Yulduz-gol as well as in its tributaries, but only of two kinds:[6] *Dyptichus*, a foot or a little over in length, and gudgeon. About half-way down this river, and for some distance on either side, are marshes (sasi) and lakelets. Here we found in the latter half of September numbers of migrating water-fowl;[7] most of the other birds nesting in this country had taken wing for the south, and it was only now and then that we saw a few in the mountains.[8] Non-migratory birds[9] however are common.

[5] This range, as well as the northern, has no general name among the inhabitants, who distinguish parts by specific names.

[6] At all events, we did not catch any other kind of fish, either in autumn or in spring, on our return journey.

[7] Common wild duck, gadwall, teal, red-crested pochard, red-headed pochard, and garrot.

[8] Redstart, accentor, mountain finch, and Brandt's finch (*Leucosticte Brandtii*) the two last-mentioned generally in flocks.

[9] Snow vulture, black vulture, wall creeper, rock partridge; and shore-lark (*Otocoris albigula*) on the steppes.

Yulduz is very rich in mammalia; of the larger animals there are brown and tawny bears, Ovis Poli, wild goat, and what are more remarkable, considering the absence of trees, deer and pygargs; numbers of marmot hybernate as early as the middle of September, when they frequently become the prey of the bear, who grubs up their burrows, and extracts from them the half-dormant little animals. Wolves are very common, and foxes particularly so; the latter prey on the innumerable field-mice. Amongst others of the rodent order, Siberian marmot are plentiful, but they were also hybernating, and wild boar are occasionally found in the marshes of the Baga Yulduz-gol.

There are absolutely no inhabitants in either Yulduz, although not above eleven years ago Turgutes lived here to the number of ten thousand kebitkas. Plundered by the Dungans, these nomads retired, partly to Shikho, and partly to the Kaidu-gol to the neighbourhood of Kara-shahr; while some escaped to our lines on the Ili, where they are living at the present day.

Our entrance into Yulduz was marked by an unfortunate incident. My companion Lieut. Povalo-Schweikofsky, who from the very first was unable to support the hardships of travel, fell ill, and as he did not recover, was obliged to return to his former place of service. Fortunately my other travelling-companion, the volunteer Eklon, proved to be an energetic and willing youth, and with a little practice he soon became an invaluable assistant.

We stayed about three weeks in Yulduz, hunting most of the time, and succeeded in obtaining about a dozen fine skins for our collection, including two males of the Ovis Poli. This magnificent sheep, characteristic of and peculiar to the highlands of Central Asia, is often seen here in herds of thirty to forty.

These herds are mostly composed of females, and a few young, full-grown males, acting as leaders and protectors. The old males[1] hold aloof, and generally roam about singly, or in twos and threes. The favourite resort of these sheep are the spurs of the great ranges, and the smooth slopes leading to the level steppe. They rarely assemble in stern, rocky mountains, where the wild goat[2] makes his home, and where the latter may also be seen in herds numbering forty and upwards, similar in habits to the arkari, and extremely difficult of approach, both on account of his wariness, as well as from the nature of the localities he frequents.

---

[1] The horns of these old males are of colossal proportions. Those in my collection measure 4 feet 8 inches in length, taking the outside of the curve, and are $1\frac{1}{2}$ feet thick at the base, their weight is about 36 lbs.

[2] In all probability this is *Capra Skyn*, not *Capra Sibirica*, the horns approaching at the tips and turning inwards; the colour of the hair is a tawny-grey, belly white. The longest horns I saw measured 4 feet.

The deer we saw in Yulduz belong to the same kind as those inhabiting the forests of the Tian Shan. The stags are of enormous size; the does are smaller, but fully equal to the full-grown male of the European deer (*Cervus elaphus*).[3] Owing to the absence of forests in Yulduz, the deer frequent the belts of low bushes, climbing the rocks as easily as the mountain sheep, and so like these as to be mistaken for them at a distance. In spring, during the months of May and June, they are eagerly pursued by hunters for the sake of their young horns—so called '*panti*,' which fetch high prices in China. Thus, in Kulja, a pair of large, six-pointed antlers is worth fifty to seventy roubles, in first hands; and even small ones fetch fifteen, twenty, or thirty roubles. The profits derived from this chase induce Russian and native hunters to pursue it with ardour during the spring, throughout the vast expanse of Asia, from Turkestan to the sea of Japan.[4]

After we had done hunting we turned into the Kaidu valley, crossing the southern slope of the Tian Shan. The ascent of the pass from the Yulduz side is so gradual as to be hardly per-

[3] A two-year old buck killed by me on Yulduz, measured 6 feet 1 inch in length, 4 feet 3 inches in height at the shoulders. A full-grown doe, killed in the same place, measured 7 feet 4 inches in length from the nose to the tail, and stood 4 feet 3 inches from the ground.

[4] Compare *Mongolia*, i. 170.

ceptible, although the elevation above sea-level is at least 9300 feet. But the descent on the other side is extremely difficult. For about forty versts the barely-distinguishable track follows the defile of the Habtsagai, and for twenty-two versts further that of the Balgantai river. Both these ravines are exceedingly narrow (in places not more than 400 feet wide), their beds strewn with *débris* of rock and pebbles, and their sides walled by huge precipitous cliffs.

The banks of the streams are thickly covered with willow and tamarisk bushes; lower down, at an elevation of about 6000 feet, buckthorn and elms appear; and, still lower, barberry and oleaster; the only grasses found in the ravines are lasiogrostis and reeds. The surrounding mountains are entirely bereft of vegetation, the neighbouring desert having affixed the seal of death on this side of the Tian Shan. Atmospheric precipitations, although plentiful on the northern side of the range where the rain-clouds deposit their moisture, the last drops of which are wrung out by the snow mountains of cold Yulduz, are absent here, and it is exceedingly probable that the whole southern slope of the Eastern Tian Shan is arid and barren.

Upon entering the Kaidu valley we descended to 3400 feet above sea level. The weather became warm, and the morning frosts no longer severe; whilst in Yulduz, towards the end of

September, the thermometer marked 10° Fahr. at
sunrise, and snow fell occasionally.

At the camping-ground of Kara-moto, where
we halted, we were well received by the first
Turgute inhabitants that we met. Meanwhile,
the report spread rapidly of the approach of the
Russians, and alarmed the whole Mohammedan
population of the neighbourhood. It was stated
that Russian troops were marching into this
country, and that their advance-guard had
already appeared on the Kaidu. This story
gained currency when, on our first arrival, the
reports of our fire-arms, as we shot pheasants
and other birds, began to be heard, and caused
such a panic among the Mohammedans living near
Kara-moto as to induce them to leave their homes
and fly to Kara-shahr.

Thither notice was of course at once sent of our
arrival, but, at first, none of the officials made
their appearance. We now sent back to Kulja
our guide Tokhta-akhoond, a man devoted to us,
but for this very reason hateful to the Mohammedans, he being himself a follower of the
prophet born at Korla, whence he had escaped
some years previously to Ili. With him we
despatched the greater part of our collections,
so as not to encumber ourselves needlessly with
them.

On the third day of our appearance at Kara-
moto, six Mohammedan envoys from the go-

vernor of Korla[5] came to inquire the object of our
journey. I explained to them that we were on
our way to Lob-nor, and that Yakub Beg was well
aware of this.[6] On receiving my reply the envoys returned to Korla, but a small picket was
stationed on the opposite bank of the Kaidu, to
watch our movements. The day afterwards the
same envoys reappeared, reporting that the governor had despatched a courier to Yakub Beg,[7] and
that until his answer were received, no permission
could be given us to proceed. This decision did
not disturb us in the least, as the wooded
country on the Kaidu abounded in wintering
birds and pheasants. The latter probably belong
to a new species, very closely allied to *Phasianus
Shawii*, recently discovered in the neighbourhood
of Kashgar by the British mission to Eastern
Turkestan, and occurring along the whole length
of the Tarim, and on Lake Lob.

The Kaidu river is from 200 to 270 feet wide
at Kara-moto, with a very rapid stream and a depth
of three to four feet at the fords, which, during
summer, are entirely impassable. Fish are plentiful in the river, but I cannot say of what kinds,
for neither in going nor coming had we the

[5] This town is fifty versts south-east of Kara-shahr.

[6] Before our departure from Kulja, Yakub Beg wrote in
answer to the Governor-General of Turkestan that the Russians going to Lob-nor would be hospitably received in his
dominions.

[7] Who was then at Toksum, not far from Turfan.

opportunity of catching any. Fish too are said to abound in Lake Bagarash, into which the Kaidu empties. This lake lies not far to the west* of Kara-shahr, and is very large and deep.[*] It would have been very interesting to have explored it; but, alas, we could not manage this, either in going or returning.

After a halt of seven days at Kara-moto, we at length received permission to proceed to the town of Korla (but not to Kara-shahr), through which lies the road to Lob-nor. The distance from Kara-moto to Korla is sixty-two versts, and we accomplished it in three days, escorted by the same men who had a little while back first visited us. At each station on the road they brought us a sheep and some fruit. Before Korla could be reached, it was necessary to cross the last spur of the Tian Shan by a defile, through which rushes the Koncheh-daria, flowing out of Bagarash into the Tarim. At either end of this defile, which is ten versts long and very narrow, stands a mud fort, garrisoned by a small force.

No sooner had we arrived at Korla, and established ourselves in a house prepared for us outside the town, than a guard was placed over us, on the plea of protecting us; but, in reality, to prevent any of the townspeople, who are extremely dissatisfied with Yakub Beg's rule, from communi-

[*] According to the Kalmuks, it is eight or nine days' ride round Bagarash.

cating with us; and, in the same way, they forbad our entering the town, for they said, "You are our honoured guests, and must not be troubled with anything; all you want, we will bring you." But these honeyed words were mere phrases; they certainly brought us a sheep, bread, and fruit daily, but here their hospitality ended. All that could interest us, or advance the objects of our journey, was denied us; and we were not allowed to know anything beyond the gate of our enclosure. To all our questions as to the town of Korla, the number of its inhabitants, their trade, the features of the surrounding country, &c., we received the curtest replies, or absolute falsehoods; and this continued during the whole of our six months' stay in the dominions of Yakub Beg, or, "*Badaulat*," i. e. the happy one, as he is termed by his subjects. Nor was it until afterwards on the Tarim and Lob-nor, that we succeeded in occasionally eliciting some information in a quiet way from the inhabitants, who, though generally well disposed, feared showing their feelings. From the people on the Tarim, we learned that Korla and its neighbouring district numbers about six thousand inhabitants of both sexes. The town itself consists of two parts, each surrounded with mud walls: the old commercial town, and the new fort occupied only by troops, of whom very few were left at the time of our visit, most of them having departed for Toksum, where Yakub Beg was superintending the erection of fortifications, to protect himself against the Chinese.

The day following our arrival at Korla one of Badaulat's personal suite, a certain Zaman Beg, formerly a Russian subject, born at Nukha[9] in Trans-Caucasia, and probably of Armenian extraction, paid us a visit. Having been actually at one time in the Russian service he spoke Russian fluently, and at once informed us that he had been sent by Badaulat to accompany us to Lob-nor—a piece of news that disconcerted us not a little, for I well knew that he was sent as a spy on our movements, and that his presence would be rather embarrassing than otherwise. Zaman Beg was, however, personally disposed to be friendly, and showed us all the attentions he could, for which I cannot be too grateful. Indeed, we got on better with him at Lob-nor than with any other of Yakub Beg's officials.

We left Korla for Lob-nor on the 4th of November. Besides the members of our own party the caravan included Zaman Beg, his servants, and a *hadji*. Hardly had we started than our companions showed us how disagreeable they

---

[9] [Nukha rose to be a place of some note about the middle of the eighteenth century, when it was the capital and place of residence of the khans of Shekin, who are reported to have turned back Nadir Shah's victorious army. In 1805 Nukha was taken by the Russian general Nebolsin, and finally annexed by Russia in 1819.—M.]

could make themselves. In order to prevent us seeing the town they led us by a circuitous path across the fields and were bare-faced enough to assure us that there was no better road. However, there was no help for it but to feign ignorance, as we also did on many subsequent occasions, however distasteful such a line of conduct was to persons like ourselves engaged in scientific inquiries of the highest importance. They suspected and deceived us at every step.; the inhabitants were forbidden to hold any intercourse with or even to speak to us. We were in fact under *surveillance*, and our escort nothing but spies. Zaman Beg evidently felt the irksomeness of the situation at times, but he could not alter his demeanour towards us. Eventually at Lobnor, when they became tired of watching us, their former distrust wore off a little, but at first the police inspection was of the strictest, and not a week passed but that a courier arrived either from Badaulat or the Tokhsabai " to inquire after our well-being," as Zaman Beg naively expressed it.

Everything tended to show that our journey to Lob-nor did not please Yakub Beg, though he could not refuse General Kauffmann, and a quarrel with Russia on the eve of a war with China would have been impolitic on his part.·

Probably with the view of inducing us to renounce our further journey, they led us to the Tarim by the most difficult road, obliging us to

cross two large and deep streams—the Koncheh
and Inchikeh-daria—by swimming. Reference to
the map will show how easily we might have kept
along the right bank of the former without having
to cross it twice unnecessarily. We could only
suppose that they wished to exaggerate the difficulties of the route by obliging us to swim in
frosty weather with the thermometer at 4° Fahr.
at sunrise. The crossing of both these streams
was satisfactorily accomplished, though the camels
suffered seriously from their cold-water bath, and
when our guides convinced themselves of the
hopelessness of their attempts to thwart us, they
set to work and constructed rafts and landing-
stages at the crossings.

Before reaching Lake Lob we had to march
due south and strike the valley of the Tarim at a
point eighty-six versts distant from Korla. For
some way the country has the appearance of an
undulating plain covered with a pebbly or gravelly
soil, and totally devoid of vegetation, forming a
belt twenty to twenty-five versts wide, more or less,
running parallel to and at the foot of the Kurugh-
tagh, a low, waterless, and barren range forming
the last arm of the Tian Shan in the direction of
the Lob-nor desert. This range, as we are told,
rises on the southern shore of Lake Bagarash, and
after continuing for nearly two hundred versts to
the east of Korla merges in the low clay or sand
hillocks of the desert.

Beyond the stony margin lying next to the mountains, and as it appears to me distinctly defining the shore-line of an ancient sea, lies the boundless expanse of the Tarim and Lob-nor deserts. Here the soil is loose saline loam or drift-sand remarkable for the absence of organic life. The Lob-nor desert is indeed the wildest and most barren of all the deserts I have seen, surpassing in this respect even that of Ala-shan.[1] But before proceeding to a more detailed description of these places, I will briefly sketch the hydrography of the Lower Tarim.

As already stated, on our road from Korla to the south we had to cross two streams of considerable size—the Koncheh-daria[2] and Inchikeh-daria. The first of these flows out of Lake Ba-garash, forces its way through the last spur of the Tian Shan near Korla, and after taking a slight bend to the south, flows in a south-easterly direction, and falls into the Kiok-ala-daria, an arm of the Tarim. Owing to the velocity of their current and the loose clay soil through which they pass, the Koncheh-daria as well as the Tarim and all its arms and tributaries have worn for themselves deep trough-like channels. The width of the Koncheh-daria where we crossed it for the second

---

[1] For a description of Ala-shan see the author's last work, *Mongolia*, &c. vol. i. ch. vi.

[2] Incorrectly marked on existing maps, both as to name and direction.

time is fifty to seventy feet; depth ten to fourteen, and even more in places. Less than ten versts to the south of the Koncheh-daria, the Inchikeh-daria lay across our road ; the latter river after a short course to the east loses itself in salt-marshes, perhaps uniting with the Koncheh at high water. After many inquiries we ascertained the Inchikeh to be an arm of the Ugen-daria, which falls into the Tarim close by, after rising in the Muzart and flowing past the towns of Bai and Sairam. In the meridian of the town of Bugur an arm sepa-rates from the Ugen-daria, uniting with the Tarim on the right, and a little further down the In-chikeh-daria branches off to the left.

We struck the Tarim at the point where it is joined by the Ugen-daria with a stream 56 to 70 feet wide. The Tarim itself is here a considerable river from 350 to 400 feet wide, with a depth of not less than twenty feet. Its water is clear and stream very rapid. The river flows in one chan-nel, and at this point reaches its furthest northing; hence it continues in a south-easterly course, then almost due south and before finally emptying into Lob-nor debouches in Lake Kara-buran. The natives rarely make use of the name Tarim in speaking of this river, which is more generally known as the Yarkand-Tarim or Yarkand-daria, after its principal feeder the river of Yarkand. The name Tarim, as we were told, is derived from " tara," i. e. field, owing to the circumstance of the water of this river in its upper course being mostly utilized to irrigate the fields.

Fifty versts below the mouth of the Ugen-daria a large arm, the Kiok-ala-daria (about 150 feet wide) separates from the Tarim and flows in an independent channel for about 130 versts before reuniting with the parent river. Into this arm flows the Koncheh-daria from the north.

With the exception of the Kiok-ala-daria the Tarim has no important subsidiary channels in its lower course, and is mostly contained in one channel. Along its banks to the right and left of its course are scattered marshes and lakes. These are for the most part artificially formed by the natives for purposes of fishing and pasturage—reeds being the only food for cattle in this wretched country. The river itself assists in the irrigation of its own valley. Fine sand and dust driven by the wind-storms prevalent in spring are caught and retained by the trees, bushes, and cane-brake growing on the banks, so as gradually to raise their level above that of the adjacent land, which is constantly diminishing under the influence of the same causes. Hence it becomes only necessary to bore through the bank for the water to pour out of the river and inundate a more or less extensive tract of plain. With the water come fish, and in a little while reeds begin to grow. After a time the channel gets silted up, the lake grows shallower, the fish are

easily taken, and the recently submerged land
affords pasturage for sheep. When the reeds are
all fed off, the operation is repeated, and a fresh
supply of fish and pasturage obtained.

The general character of the Lower Tarim is
very much as we have described it. Along the
right bank and not far from the river lie bare
hillocks of drift-sand twenty to sixty feet high.
These sandy wastes continue the whole way down
the Tarim to its confluence with Lake Kara-buran,
then up the Cherchen-daria in a south-westerly
direction, almost as far as the town of Keria,
and a long way up the Tarim from the mouth of
the Ugen-daria. Indeed the whole country between the right bank of the Tarim on the one
side to the oases at the foot of the Kuen-lun on
the other is described to be filled with drift-sand
and positively uninhabitable.

On the left bank of the Tarim the sands are
much less frequent and not nearly so extensive.
Here the soil consists of loose saline clay in some
places entirely bare, in others again overgrown
with rare bushes of tamarisk and occasionally
patches of Haloxylon. These plants bind the
yielding soil with their roots, the intervals being
subjected to the full force of the wind, which
accumulates the drift round the bushes so as
gradually to form a hillock seven to fourteen feet
high beneath each of them; and such hillocks cover
vast areas, as they do in Ordos and Alashan.

On the banks of the Tarim itself, as well as on its arms and tributaries, vegetation is somewhat more varied, though scanty in the extreme. First of all, in the narrow wooded belt we notice the poplar (*Populus diversifolia*) a crooked tree attaining a height of between twenty-five to thirty-five feet, with an almost invariably hollow trunk from one to three feet thick; the oleaster in small quantities; the *Halimodendron, Asclepias,* and two other kinds of bushes of the bean family, covering vast areas, whilst tall cane-brake and *Typha* obstruct the lakes and marshes on both banks of the Tarim, and as a rarity, wild pea and Astragalus, with two or three representatives of the genus *Compositæ* growing here and there on the damper ground. These complete the list of plants of the Tarim and Lob-nor.[3] No meadows, no grass, not a vestige of a flower is here to be seen.

It would indeed be difficult to picture to oneself a more desolate landscape; the poplar woods, with their bare soil, covered only in autumn with fallen leaves parched and shrivelled with the dry heat, withered branches and prostrate trees encumbering the ground, cane-brake crackling under foot, and saline dust ready to envelope you

---

[3] Moreover the poplar and elæagnus only grow along the Tarim, not on Lob-nor. [Henderson remarks that the latter is one of the most common trees in Yarkand, where it is cultivated as a tall hedge and for its fruit along roadsides. (*Lahore to Yarkand*, p. 335). The name is derived from ἐλαία, an olive, the tree having a striking resemblance to an olive-tree.—M.]

from every bough that you brush aside from your path.[4] Now, again, you come to acres of dead poplars, with broken boughs, shorn of their bark, lifeless trunks never decaying, but crumbling away by degrees, to be hidden in layers of sand.

But cheerless as these woods are, the neighbouring desert is even more dreary. Nothing can exceed the monotony of the scenery. Whichever way you turn, an ill-favoured plain meets your eye, covered with what seem to be large mounds, but which are really hillocks of clay surmounted by tamarisk, between which the path winds, every surrounding object shut out from sight, and even the distant hills barely visible in blue outline through the dusty vapour which fills the atmosphere like fog. Not a bird, not an animal, nothing but the occasional tracks of the timid gazelle.

[4] The poplars are so saturated with salt that on breaking a bough a saline incrustation may be seen on the wood.

CHAPTER II.

Fauna of Tarim—Avi-fauna—New species—Inhabitants of
Tarim—Rude dwellings—Details of population—Dress of
the people—Cloth manufacture—Habits, pursuits, and
diet—Position of their women—Peculiarities and failings—
Route continued—Observations for altitude—Natives are
suspicious—Airilgan ferry—Climate—Village of Chargalyk
—Cherchen, Nai, and Keria—Ruins of Lob—Starovertsi—
Start for Altyn-tagh—Description of these mountains—
Mountainous system—Fauna of Altyn-tagh—Hardships
—Return to Lob.

LET us now turn to the animal kingdom. It may
be seen from the preceding brief sketch that the
basin of the Lower Tarim and Lake Lob contain
little for the support of mammalia. Of these we
give a complete list in the appendix, and merely
remark here that this country is in general as
deficient in the variety, as it is in the number of
its mammals. Wild boar and hares excepted, all
other animals are comparatively few, and some
very scarce. This fauna, too, has no distinguishing feature, for, excepting the wild camel, most of
the animals are also found in the Tian Shan,
whilst the remainder are common to the deserts of
Central Asia generally.

Neither is the country we are describing rich
in birds, although one might have supposed that

the woods and warm climate in the Tarim valley would have attracted many to winter here. Their absence, however, may be accounted for by the want of food, for, with the exception of oleaster, and even this in comparatively small quantities, there is not a single bush or herb with edible seeds. Fish, mollusca, and other small animals common to lakes and marshes, are beyond the reach of birds in winter. This is why neither waterfowl nor wading birds [1] winter on the Tarim; birds of prey are also scarce, and only one songster appears in any number in winter, viz. the black-throated thrush [2] (*Turdus atrigularis*); of the *Columbidæ* we observed three kinds in winter, not on the Tarim, however, but at Chargalyk, forty versts to the S. E. of Lake Kara-buran.

Most of the birds, of which a list will be found in the Appendix, were also observed by us in the valley of the Kaidu and near the town of Korla. Besides these we found *Corvus frugilegus, C.*

[1] In the end of November, however, we met with single specimens of *Carbo cormoranus, Anas clypeata, Harelda glacialis, Larus brunneicephalus*, but these had probably been left behind by their fellows, and perhaps would have taken their departure later. Besides these in Lob-nor itself, as the natives informed us, *Botaurus stellaris*, and *Cygnus olor* occasionally winter amongst the reeds where the frost does not penetrate.

[2] [Blanford found the black-throated thrush, common in Báluchistán in winter, as well as in the " miserable apologies for gardens at Gwádar, one of the most desolate of inhabited spots on the earth's surface."—(Cf. *Eastern Persia*, vol. ii., zoology, p. 158.)—M.]

monedula, Coturnix communis, Cynchramus polaris,
Columba rupestris, Perdix daurica, Caccabis chukar,
the three last named being peculiar to the mountains. Many more birds must, in my opinion,
winter in the oases at the foot of the Tian Shan,
where food is more abundant than on the Tarim
and Lob-nor.

Of the forty-eight varieties of birds observed in
winter on the Tarim, two are new species. Of
these one named by me, *Rhopophilus deserti*, was
also seen during my last expedition to Tsaidam.
Having on that occasion only obtained two or
three specimens, I decided not to form a separate
species, but to call them a variety of *Rhopophilus
pekinensis Swinh. var. major.* But now that I am
convinced from a number of specimens of the constant recurrence of certain marks (greater size
and pale-coloured plumage) distinguishing the
Central Asian bird from its Chinese congener, I
have distinguished it as a new species, under the
name of " *deserti*," for it is characteristic of the
desert, and is neither found north of the Tian Shan,
nor in Russian Turkestan.

Another very interesting novelty among the
birds of the Tarim, is a new *Podoces*. Hitherto
we only knew of three species[3] of this sub-genus.
A fourth has now been added, which I have
named *Podoces tarimensis*.[4] The new Podoces

[3] *Podoces Panderi, P. Hendersoni, P. humilis.*
[4] I. e. of or belonging to the Tarim, where it was first dis-

does not differ in its habits from the closely-allied
P. Hendersoni,[5] and its range does not extend to
the north of the Tian Shan, or into Russian
Turkestan.

Of fish, only two kinds are known in the Tarim
as well as in Lob-nor itself; the *Marœna,* and
another (of the carp family) strange to me.[6]
Both are very numerous, especially the former,
and they constitute the chief sustenance of the
inhabitants.

Population is first met on descending the
Tarim, at the mouth of the Ugen-daria; for
administrative purposes the people are divided
into two districts—the Tarimtsi or Kara-Kultsi,[7]
and the Lobnortsi proper or Kara-Kurchintsi.[8]
Let us say a few words concerning the former;
we shall speak of the Kara-Kurchintsi later, in
describing Lob-nor.

---

covered, and to the basin of which river it appears exclusively to
belong. [Since I began this translation, Col. Prejevalsky has
informed me that the new species of Podoces mentioned in the
text, has been identified as *P. Biddulphii,* discovered during Sir
D. Forsyth's expedition to Kashgar.—M.]

[5] [This bird appears to bear a closer resemblance to the
chough than to any other, and Shaw said that they were good
eating. See *Lahore to Yarkand,* p. 244.—M.]

[6] We have several excellent specimens of Lob-nor and Tarim
fish in our collection.

[7] After Lake Kara-Kul, near which lives an akhoond who
governs the people on the Lower Tarim.

[8] More correctly Kara-Koshuntsi from the word Kara-
Koshun, i.e. black district or quarter.

We were informed that the present inhabitants
on the Tarim originally lived at Lake Lob; but
that a hundred years ago, owing to a scarcity of
fish, and Kalmuk raids, they became dispersed
along the banks of the Tarim. We could not
ascertain whether, in earlier times, this river's
banks were inhabited; one thing, however, is
certain, that fugitives, and perhaps exiles, from
different parts of Eastern Turkestan, were continually intermixing with the settlers from Lake
Lob. Hence the Tarimtsi of the present day,
originally doubtless of the Aryan race, have a
curiously mixed type of features, and among them
may be seen the physiognomy of Sarts, Kirghizes,
and even Tangutans; now and then a thoroughly
European face will attract your attention, or one
characteristic of the Mongolian.

These natives are in general all remarkable for
the pallor of their complexions, for their hollow
chests and weak frames. The men are of average
height, many even tall; the women (whom we
rarely saw) are of smaller stature.

If we happened to enter one of their dwellings
—the fair sex, married and single, invariably took
to flight, disappearing like mice through the
crevices of their reed walls.

Our companion, Zaman Beg, having had more
opportunities of seeing and studying the ladies on
the Tarim, spoke in terms the reverse of flattering
of their beauty. One fair one he did except from

F

his category, and she came from the village of
Akhtarma, and was described as presenting a
striking anomaly among her black-haired and
dark-eyed countrywomen.　She may probably
have been a memento of the visit of some Russian
starovertsi in 1862, of whom we shall say something presently.

As to the language, I can only say that our
interpreter, a Taranchi from Kulja, had no difficulty in making himself understood on all parts
of the Tarim and Lob-nor.　Hence it may be
inferred that the distinction between the Taranchi
and Sart languages on the one hand, and the dialect spoken by the natives of these parts on the
other is slight.　Being myself ignorant of any of
these forms of speech, I was unable personally to
make any observations upon them, and the interpreter was too stupid to assist me.

The religion of all these people is Mohammedan, with a slight admixture of heathenish
rites.　For instance, they always bury their dead
in canoes, and dispose the fishing-nets of the
deceased round his grave.

Their dwelling-places are made of reeds which
grow in abundance on the marshes and lakes of
the Tarim valley.　These habitations are constructed in the most primitive fashion.　Round,
rough poplar poles are first driven into the
ground at the corners and sides; to these are
fastened cross-beams and rods to support the

ceiling. The sides are covered with reeds fastened
in some way together, and the ceiling is also of
the same material, a square hole being left for the
escape of smoke. In the centre of this apartment
stands the fireplace; along the walls, on mats of
felt or reed, the master and his family sleep,
separate quarters being in some cases reserved
for the women. On shelves fastened to the walls,
are disposed the domestic utensils, &c. Close
beside the habitation is an enclosure also of reeds
for the cattle. Ten or more of such houses com-
pose the village, which is not always stationary,
for in winter they live wherever food for cattle
and fuel are most abundant, whilst in summer
they are dispersed over the lake for the purpose
of fishing. But their chief motive in removing
their villages to new sites is to avoid sickness;
small-pox is especially dreaded, for it almost
invariably terminates fatally. Any one falling ill
of this complaint is abandoned to his fate; a
little food is left by the side of the sick man, and
the whole village decamps to another place, without further thought for their deserted brother.
If he recover, which seldom happens, he returns
to his relatives; in the contrary event, nobody
troubles himself to bury him. Such of the graves
as we saw were marked with long poles, decorated
with coloured rags, deers' horns, wild yak tails, &c.[*]

[*] The wild yak inhabits the mountains to the south of Lob-
nor.

The inhabitants on the Lower Tarim number 1200 of both sexes. The following is a list of their villages,[1] with details of population :—

Villages.	Houses.	Men.	Women.	Children.	Total.
Kutmet-kul	6	10	14	18	42
Akhtarma	35	103	120	88	311
Taiz-kul	15	47	52	34	133
Kara-kyr	14	38	30	40	108
Kiok-ala	30	93	109	61	263
Markat	14	58	49	61	168
Uiman-kul	6	20	18	18	56
Ehni-su	12	38	23	30	91
Airilgan	4	6	4	2	12
Total	136	413	419	352	1184

The dress of the Tarimtsi consists of a camel's hair coat and trousers, a long shirt underneath, and a sheepskin cloak in winter,—a few, but these are exceptions, and only the most prosperous, wear the khalat and turban. The rich have shoes, the poor—sandals of their own make, fastened over felt stockings in winter ; in summer their feet are bare. Their head-dress in winter is a lambskin cap turned up at the brim, in summer a felt hat.

The women wear a short khalat with girdle like

---

[1] The villages are here given in regular order, beginning from the mouth of the Ugen-daria, and descending the Tarim to Lake Kara-buran.

that of the men, but unlike these, they always leave it unfastened; underneath is a shirt; the trousers are tucked into boots like men's. Their head-dress is also a fur cap, beneath which is a white cloth flowing over the back, two ends being frequently tied under the chin. The men shave the entire head; the women braid their back hair into two tresses, allowing the front locks to fall half way down the cheeks, and keeping them cut to this length. Unmarried girls have only one tress behind. They obtain most of their wearing apparel and domestic utensils from the Korla merchants; some are of home make. The cloth is prepared from sheep's wool, or the fibre of the Asclepias plant, growing in abundance in the Tarim valley. In autumn and winter they collect the withered stalks of this plant, and after beating it with sticks, or with the hand, in order to separate the fibre, they boil it in water, cleanse and boil it a second time; after which it undergoes the final process of combing. The distaff used for spinning is of a peculiar kind, and the yarn thus obtained is woven, by means of a primitive loom and shuttle, into cloth of a very durable texture, not inelegantly decorated.

This cloth-manufacture and the preparation of wild beasts' skins are their only industry, although blacksmiths and bootmakers are occasionally found among them.

Their chief occupation is fishing, and fish constitutes their staple food. The nets they use are small and coarsely made. We shall describe their mode of fishing later, suffice it to say here that their lives are mostly passed on the water, and that they are expert in the management of their canoes, both men and women excelling in the art. The canoes are made of hollowed poplar-trees, and form an indispensable adjunct to every household. Their fish diet is varied by Asclepias root, roasted on the fire and eaten instead of bread— the latter being a delicacy reserved only for the very few rich among them. Agriculture is very backward on the Lower Tarim, and was only introduced here, as we heard, about ten years ago. Before sowing, the soil has to be irrigated by artificial dykes. Wheat and barley in small quantities are sown, but the harvest is never particularly good, owing to the saline nature of the soil. Cattle rearing is more general than agriculture. Sheep are the principal domestic animals, and yield an excellent fleece; but they are small, and of the fat-tailed kind; horned cattle of a fine, large breed, a few horses, and asses are also kept. Of camels there are none, the locality disagreeing with them. The reeds we have already mentioned are the only fodder for cattle, but sheep greedily devour besides the stalks of a prickly bush.

With regard to the moral side of the inhabitants of the Tarim, their chief characteristic, as with

Asiatics in general, is laziness; and, next to this, dissimulation and suspicion; fanaticism does not run high here, and their family life is probably the same as that of other Turkestanis. The wife is mistress of her household, but at the same time her husband's slave, and he may turn her out whenever he chooses and take another, or keep several wives at a time. Marriage may be contracted for the shortest period, even though only for a few days. Their most peculiar habit is that of talking loudly, and with great rapidity of utterance; so much so, that on hearing them conversing with one another, a stranger might suppose that they were quarrelling. Their expression of astonishment is by smacking their lips, and exclaiming "Toba, Toba." For administrative purposes these people, together with the Lobnortsi, are under the governor of Korla, to whom they pay taxes.

To return to our narrative, after this long digression. Having crossed, in the way we have described, the Koncheh and Inchikeh rivers, we struck the Tarim at the point of its confluence with the Ugen-daria, whence another day's march brought us to Akhtarma,[1] the largest of all the settlements on the Tarim and Lob-nor, and the residence of Akhoond Aehliam, governor of Tarim,

---

[1] Not far from this village, on the opposite side of the Tarim, lies Lake Kara-kul, which has given its name to the inhabitants of the Tarim valley.

who, notwithstanding his high-sounding title, signifying, as Zaman Beg informed us, "most learned of
men," is quite illiterate. Here we halted eight days,
and took astronomical observations for longitude
and barometrical measurements of altitude, finding
the latter to be 2500 feet[3] above sea-level. The
height of Lake Lob is 2200 feet, and therefore
the fall of the Tarim, notwithstanding its rapid
stream averaging three feet per second,[4] is only
slight.

From Akhtarma our road lay down the Tarim,
now approaching its bank, now retreating to some
distance from it. There is no valley in our sense
of the word; neither the configuration nor quality
of the soil changes even on the very bank of the
river. The same loamy plain, the same drift-sand
as in the desert, continue to within a hundred
paces of the water. The very limited belt of irrigated land[5] is only denoted by the marginal belts
of trees, thick reeds in some places, or marshes
and lakes in others. Travelling here with camels
is extremely difficult, for you have to pass now
through woods, or thick, prickly jungle; now

[3] Korla is 2600 feet above sea-level.

[4] I take the mean of two measurements, one early in December below the mouth of the Kiok-ala-daria, the other in March
near Lake Lob. The former gave 3·2 per second, the latter
2·83.

[5] The valley of the Tarim, however, from the mouth of the
Ugen-daria to the village of Akhtarma is distinctly defined; it
is five or six versts wide, and marshy almost throughout.

through withered canebrake, whose roots, as hard as iron, lacerate the camel's hoofs till they bleed.

After crossing the Kiok-ala-daria, an arm of the Tarim, by means of a raft, we continued to make short marches, halting generally near the villages. Zaman Beg and his suite never left us at first; but at length, having convinced themselves that we had no particular object in view, they would generally ride forward to the next halting-place.

The inhabitants on our line of march had evidently been instructed to deceive us in everything that we could not see for ourselves; and never before having set eyes on Russians, about whom they had probably heard marvellous tales, they fled as though we had the plague, and to the very last suspected us of dishonesty, seeing that we, "the valued guests" of their ruler, were treated as spies, and led by circuitous roads in charge of an escort; their suspicions too were heightened, owing to their not understanding the object of our journey. Just as it happened to us in Mongolia and Kansuh, so now on the Tarim, the semi-barbarous natives could not believe it possible that we should undergo the hardships of travel, spend money, sacrifice camels, &c., merely for the sake of seeing a new country, collecting plants and skins, &c., objects which from their point of view were good for little, if not absolutely worthless. Animated by this spirit, the eagerness

of the Tarimtsi to deceive us often went beyond
all bounds, and became childish and silly.

The only person who would tell us the truth
was Zaman Beg. But his knowledge of the
language was deficient, and he was often the dupe
of the natives, who suspected him of being friendly
to the Russians.

The sheep supplied to us during the march
were taken from the inhabitants, and nothing
would induce them to accept payment. As some
return for these acts of spoliation, I caused 100
roubles to be distributed among the poor of Lob-
nor. On the Tarim, however, positive orders had
been given not to take money, and the Akhoond
of the district assured me that he had no poor.

After marching 190 versts down the Tarim from
the mouth of the Ugen-daria, we reached the place
where the Kiok-ala-daria reunites with the main
stream. Here we crossed the Tarim a second time
on a raft, at a place called Airilgan, where the
river is 100 feet wide, and 21 feet deep.[*] After
receiving the Kiok-ala-daria, the Tarim again
increases, its width being between 210 and 245 feet,
these continue to be its dimensions until it discharges into Lake Kara-buran. Fifteen versts
above its outflow into the lake, a small square
mud fort (Kurgan) has been erected on the right

---

[*] At Airilgan ferry a boat capsized, turning one of the Cossacks and me into the river. Fortunately we swam ashore and
escaped with a ducking (10th December).

bank; in this, at the time of our journey, there
were only a few soldiers from Korla.

During the whole of our progress down the
Tarim, i. e. during the whole of November and part
of December, the weather was very fine, bright,
and warm. The night frosts were certainly as
severe as 7° Fahr.; but no sooner did the sun appear than the temperature rose rapidly, and it was
not till the 19th December that the thermometer
stood below freezing point at midday. It was probably about this time that the Tarim froze, although
perhaps not entirely. Gales were of rare occurrence, but the air was excessively dry, and filled
with vapoury dust. Of atmospherical deposits
there were none, indeed the natives say that a
snowfall is a rare occurrence in this country,
happening perhaps once or twice in three or four
winters, and thawing rapidly; rains, too, are very
unusual in summer.

From the above-mentioned mud fort we directed
our march, not towards Lob-nor, which was now
near, but due south to the village of Chargalyk,[1]
founded thirty years ago by exiles and free emigrants from Khoten. The village now consists
of twenty-one houses,[2] and a mud fort to contain

[1] The reason of our not proceeding direct to Lob-nor was that
it suited our escort's convenience to winter at Chargalyk,
and we were again deceived by the assurance that there was no
road to Lob-nor.

[2] Including nine houses of Lob-nortsi.

the exiles,[2] who are compelled to cultivate the land for Government, whilst the other inhabitants reap their own crops. The water used in irrigating the soil is led from the Chargalyk-daria, which flows from the neighbouring Altyn-tagh mountains, an elevated range south of Lob-nor.

Three hundred versts[1] to the south-west of Chargalyk, and under one governor with it, stands the small town of Cherchen,[2] on a river of the same name. Hence it is ten days' march in a south-west direction to the oasis of Nai (900 houses), and three days' further to the town of Keria, said to contain 3000 houses. From Keria there is a road to Khotan, viâ Djira, all three places being included in the territory of Kashgar.

One day's journey from Keria gold is obtained in the mountains, and other gold-mines are situated five days' march from Cherchen, near the sources of the Cherchen-daria. The quantity of gold annually produced in these mines is said to be about 19 cwt., which finds its way into Yakub Beg's treasury.

On the site of the present village of Chargalyk, remains of mud walls of an ancient city, called *Ottogush-shari*,[3] may be seen. These ruins are

---

[2] Numbering 114 of both sexes.

[1] Eleven days caravan journey.

[2] Is not this the Charchand of Marco Polo? We were told that Cherchen only contains thirty houses at present, but I cannot vouch for the accuracy of this information.

[3] I.e. the city of Ottogush, formerly Khan of this place.

reported to be two miles in circumference, and watch-towers stand in front of the principal wall. Two days' journey from Chargalyk, in the direction of Cherchen, the ruins of another ancient city called *Gas-shari* are reported to exist; and, lastly, we discovered traces of a third very large city near Lob-nor, at a place called merely *Kunia-shari*,[4] i. e. old town. We could learn of no traditions among the inhabitants respecting any of these ancient remains. Our inquiries as to the recent visit of Russian *starovertsi*[5] to Lob-nor, led to important results. Persons who had witnessed the arrival of these strangers, who doubtless came to this remote corner of Asia to seek for the promised land of "*Biélovódiye*," said of them that the first detachment to arrive at Lob-nor in 1861 numbered altogether ten men. After prospecting the locality two of their number returned, and the following year a more numerous party, consisting of 160 men and women,[6] appeared. They were all mounted on horseback, and carried their effects on pack-horses; most of the men were armed with old-fashioned muskets, and a few understood

[4] [Col. Yule is of opinion that this must be the city of Lop or Lob of Marco Polo and Mirza Haidar (see Marco Polo, ii. 201.) —M.]

[5] [Literally Old Believers; they are dissenters from the Russian Greek Church, for some account of their sects, vide chap. xx. of Wallace's *Russia*.—M.]

[6] Some said there were only seventy Russians, but the former figure is most probably correct.

how to repair the guns, and even manufacture
new ones; there were also carpenters and joiners
among them. They supplied themselves with
provisions by catching fish, and killing wild boar
by the way; but they strictly adhered to their
customs of eating no other food than that cooked
in their own utensils, and avoiding prohibited
meats.[1] They were described to be courageous
and persevering folk. Some of them settled on
the Lower Tarim, near the fort of the present day;
here they built themselves reed huts, in which
they passed the winter. Others settled at Chargalyk, where they built a wooden house, perhaps
intended to serve as a church, and this edifice has
been quite recently swept away by the floods on
the Cherchen river.

In the meanwhile a great many of the horses
of the Russians had perished—some during the
winter, and others on the journey, owing to the
difficulties of the road, improper food, and swarms
of mosquitoes. The immigrants were not pleased
with their newly adopted country, and on the
return of spring they decided on retracing their
steps or seeking a better fortune elsewhere. The
Chinese governor of Turfan, to whom Lob-nor
was then subject, gave orders to supply them
with the requisite horses and provisions; and one

---

[1] [For ecclesiastical system of Old Believers, see Duncan's
Russia, ii. 225, Herberstein in Hakluyt, vol ii., and supplementary note.—M.]

of our escort, Rakhmet Beg, was deputed to
conduct them back to Ushak-tala,[*] situated on
the road from Kara-shahr to Turfan. On reaching
the last-named place the emigrants departed for
Urumtsi, and nothing has been since heard of
them, for the outbreak of the Dungan insurrection
interrupted communications with the trans-Tian-
Shan districts. This is all we could ascertain about
the starovertsi sometime resident at Lob-nor.

After a week's rest at Chargalyk, where I left
the greater part of my baggage in charge of three
Cossacks, I started with the three other Cossacks
and my assistant, F. L. Eklon, the day after
Christmas day, for the Altyn-tagh[*] mountains to
hunt the wild camel, which according to the
unanimous testimony of the Lob-nortsi inhabits
these mountains and the deserts to the east of
them. Zaman Beg and his companions also remained behind at Chargalyk.

Our caravan now consisted of only eleven

[*] [According to Route XVI. in the Geogr. Appendix to Capt.
Trotter's Report of the survey operations in E. Turkestan,
1873-74, Ushak-tal is the third stage from Kara-shahr, on the
road to Turfan, the route from Turfan to Urumtsi is also given
(ibid. Route XVII.)—M.]

[*] [Col. Yule informs me that these mountains are described in
dry Chinese fashion, in the Chinese hydrography of the Kashgar basin, translated by Stan. Julien in the *N. Annales de
Voyages* for 1846 (vol. iii.). They seem, however, to describe
the mountains as approaching within some twenty miles of the
Tarim-gol, which we gather from this notice of Prejevalsky is
not the case.—M.]

camels and a riding-horse for me.   Eklon bestrode
a camel.   We took with us a *yurta* [felt tent]
in case of severe cold, and provisions to last six
weeks.   Our guides were two of the best hunters
of Lob-nor, in whose opinion hunting wild camels
in winter offered few chances of success.   We
nevertheless decided upon trying our luck, for we
could not defer making the attempt till spring,
having other work to do then, such as observing
the flight of birds.

Let us first describe the Altyn-tagh Mountains.
This range is first seen from the Airilgan ferry,
upwards of 100 miles off, whence it appears as an
indistinct, narrow belt, hardly remarkable above
the horizon.   After the wearisome monotony of
the Tarim valley and its adjacent desert, the
traveller greets with pleasure this range, which
gradually grows more distinct at the end of
each successive march.   Not only are the peaks
distinguishable, but the principal ravines may also
be traced, and an experienced eye can even from a
great distance detect their relative height to be
very considerable.   On arriving at Chargalyk the
Altyn-tagh appeared to us like a huge rampart
towering up even higher towards the south-west,
where it exceeded the limit of the perpetual snow
line.

We succeeded in exploring these mountains,
that is to say, their northern slopes, over an extent
of 300 versts east of Chargalyk.   Throughout the

whole of this distance the Altyn-tagh serves to
buttress a lofty plateau overhanging the Lob-nor
desert, and most probably forming the northern
limit of the Tibetan highlands ; at least this is what
the inhabitants gave us to understand, one and all
assuring us that the south-western prolongations
of the Altyn-tagh continued to margin the desert
uninterruptedly as far as the towns of Keria and
Khotan. According to the same informants this
range stretches a long way in an easterly direction, but where it terminates none could say. •

In the central part of the range where we
explored it the topography is as follows : First,
from Chargalyk to the Djagansai rivulet it stands
like a perpendicular wall above the barren, pebbly
plain, hardly if at all above the level of Lake Lob.
From Djagansai to Kurgan-bulak rivulet (and
possibly even further east), that is to say, exactly
south of the lake, the plain rises in a steep but
gradual incline [1] to the foot of the mountains,
until (at Asganlyk spring) it attains an elevation
of 7700 feet above the sea. At Kurgan-bulak
and eastward to the rivulet Djaskansai lies a
confused network of low clay hills; east of
this again hillocks of drift-sand, known under the
name of Kum-tagh are reported to extend in a
broad belt far away to the east (probably skirting
the foot of the Altyn-tagh the whole way) to
within two marches of Sha-chau.

[1] Average rise 120 feet in the verst.

On the side of the desert the Altyn-tagh throws out spurs and branches separated from one another by narrow valleys,[2] a few of which attain an elevation of 11,000 feet above sea-level. The peaks shoot up about two or three thousand feet higher, and this is probably the elevation of the main axis of the range, the descent to the table-land on the south being doubtless shorter, as we gathered not only from the testimony of our guides, but also from the general characteristics of most of the mountain ranges of Central Asia.

Although we were unable, owing to deep winter which set in and want of time, to cross to the other side of the Altyn-tagh, and measure the altitudes to the south of it, there can be no doubt of the plateau on that side being at least 12,000 or 13,000 feet above sea-level. This, at all events, may be inferred from the enormous elevation of the valleys in the front terraces of the range. Our guides, who had often hunted on the other side of these mountains, informed us that by going south along an old road, after crossing the Altyn-tagh one arrives at a lofty plain, fifty versts wide, bounded by a range (twenty versts in width) having no specific name, and beyond this again another plain, forty versts wide, abounding in morasses fed by springs (*sasi*), and confined on the south by a huge snowy

[2] Ten versts long by four and five wide, and often less.

range, the Chamen-tagh, these two valleys with
their marginal ranges continuing far beyond the
eastern horizon, whilst on the west all three
—the Altyn-tagh, the unnamed, and the Chamen-
tagh—unite not far from the town of Cherchen in
one snowy chain, Tuguz-daban, extending to the
towns of Keria and Khotan.

The natives distinguish under separate names
the two parts of the Altyn-tagh; the mountains
nearest to the desert of Lob they call Astyn-tagh
(i. e. lower hills), those farthest removed from it
towards the axis of the range, Ustiun-tagh (i. e.
upper hills).

Clay, marls, sandstone, and limestone prevail
on the outer border of Altyn-tagh, porphyry is
not uncommon in the higher parts, but granite is
rare. Water is very deficient in these mountains,
even springs are rare, and in such as are to be met
with, the water is mostly of a bitter-saline flavour.

These hills are in general characterized by extreme sterility, the scanty vegetation being confined to the upper valleys and gorges, where two
or three kinds of the prevailing low, stunted, saline
plants, three or four of the order *Compositæ*, and
dwarf bushes of *Potentilla*, *Ephedra*, &c., may
be found.

As a rarity I occasionally saw withered blossoms of *Statice* and climbing *Euonymus*. Tamarisk grows at the bottom of the ravines, reeds on
the damper ground (up to 9000 feet), here and

there may be seen *dirisun, Calligonum* and *Nit-raria*, and in a few places poplar and wild rose; the latter, however, we only found in Asganlyk ravine. Most of these plants also grow on the border of the desert nearest to the mountains, where the gnarled saksaul also appears.

It is remarkable that notwithstanding the sterility of Altyn-tagh, locusts appear in such large numbers that in the summer of 1876 they devoured all the fronds and young shoots of the reeds for want of something better to eat, and were actually found in the mountains at an elevation of 9000 feet above the sea.

The northern slope of Altyn-tagh is not rich in animal life. We were told that wild beasts were more numerous on the high plateau to the south of the range, especially below, and in the midst of the Chamen-tagh mountains. Here is a list of the mammalia of Altyn-tagh:—

Felis irbis—very rare.

Weasel, *Mustela intermedia ?*—rare.

Wolves and foxes rather scarce; the Tibetan wolf (*C. Chanko*) is reported to be seen.

Hares common in valleys; and distinct from the Lob-nor species.

Meriones, sp. in valleys—rare.

Wild camel (*Camelus Bactrianus ferus*)—rarely appears.

Ovis Poli—rare.

Mountain sheep (*Pseudo-Nahoor*)—common.

Wild yak (*Poëphagus grunniens, ferus*)—rare.

Wild ass (*Equus Kiang*)—rare.

Wild pig (*Sus scrofa ferus*) in valleys—rare.

Besides the above a species of marmot and Hodgson's antelope are reported to frequent the Chamen-tagh range.

On comparing the above list with the mammalia of the Tarim valley, it will be seen that ten kinds inhabit the Altyn-tagh (together with the Chamen-tagh) which are absent from the Tarim valley and Lob-nor. Of these, the blue mountain sheep, wild yak, and Hodgson's antelope,* are peculiar to Tibet, and here find the northern limit of their range.

Of birds there are only a few in the Altyn-tagh, as in winter we found but eighteen kinds.⁴

The climate in winter is extremely rigorous, and snow falls rarely; at all events on the northern slopes. In summer, as we were told by the hunters, rains and cold winds are of frequent occurrence.

Besides hunters' tracks, there are two roads in

---

* [For a description of these animals see *Mongolia*, by the same author, English translation, vol. i. chap. vi. and vol. ii. chap. vi.—M.]

⁴ *Gypaëtus barbatus, Vultur cinereus, Gyps himalayensis, Falco æsalon, Aquila fulva, Accentor fulvescens, Leptopciles Sophiæ, Turdus mystacinus, Linota montium, Erythrospiza mœogolica, Carpodacus rubicilla, Corvus corax, Podoces Biddulphii* (up to 10,000 feet), *Fregilus graculus, Otocoris albigula, Caccabis chukar, Megaloperdix sp., Scolopax hyemalis.*

these mountains; one leading from Lob-nor to
Tibet, the other to the town of Sha-chau,
neither of which are now used, the Kalmuks
having discontinued their pilgrimages to Tibet
since the outbreak of the Dungan insurrection.
By the Sha-chau road, however, a few years ago
some parties of Dungans succeeded in effecting
their escape from the Chinese, and it was by this
road that we pursued our journey to Chaglyk
spring; beyond which our guides knew nothing
of the country.   The path is marked at the passes
and at a few other places by piles of stones; in all
probability it continues in the Altyn-tagh Mountains for the rest of the way to Sha-chau, the
neighbouring desert being waterless.

For forty days[5] we marched at the foot of the
Altyn-tagh Mountains, and in the mountains
themselves, accomplishing a distance of exactly
500 versts; but during the whole of this time we
only saw one wild camel,[6] and this we were unable
to kill.   Of other large game we only bagged a
Kulan (wild ass) and a male yak.   Upon the
whole, then, this excursion was most unsuccessful
and full of mishaps.   At a great elevation, in mid-
winter, in the midst of an extremely barren country, we suffered most of all from scarcity of water
and frost (as severe as—16° Fahr.).   Fuel was also

---

[5] From the 26th December to the 5th February.

[6] I fired at this camel at 500 paces and missed him; a memo-
rable miss for a sportsman.

very scarce, and owing to the ill success of our shooting parties we could not obtain a sufficient supply of fresh meat, and had to live on hares for some days. At the halting-places, the loose, saline, clayey soil pulverized instantly, and covered everything in our tent with a layer of dust. We ourselves had been unable to wash for a whole week, and could not endure our dirty condition, our clothes too became saturated with dust, and our linen of a dirty chocolate colour. In fact, we were experiencing a repetition of last winter's sufferings in Northern Tibet.

After a week's halt near Chaglyk' spring, and fixing its latitude and longitude, we decided on returning to Lob-nor to observe the flight of birds, which would soon take place. Two of our guides were to return once more to the mountains to seek for wild camel, as it was indispensable that we should procure a specimen at any cost. As an additional incentive I offered a reward of 100 roubles for a male and female, being fifty times the price usually obtained for them by the native hunters.

' Hence I rode into the Kum-tagh sands after camels, but without success.

CHAPTER III.

ACCORDING to the unanimous testimony of the
Lob-nortsi, the chief habitat of the wild camel at
the present day is the desert of Kum-tagh, to the
east of Lake Lob; this animal is also occasionally
found on the Lower Tarim, in the Kuruk-tagh
mountains, and more rarely still in the sands
bordering with the Cherchen-daria; beyond the
town of Cherchen, in the direction of Khoten, its
existence is not known. Twenty years ago, wild
camels were numerous near Lake Lob, where the
village of Chargalik now stands, and farther to

the east along the foot of the Altyn-tagh, as well as in the range itself. Our guide, a hunter of Chargalik, told us that it was not unusual in those days, to see some dozens, or even a hundred of these animals together. He himself had killed upwards of a hundred of them in the course of his life (and he was an old man), with a flint and steel musket. With an increase of population at Chargalik, the hunters of Lob-nor became more numerous, and camels scarcer. Now, the wild camel only frequents the neighbourhood of Lob-nor, and even here in small numbers. Years pass without so much as one being seen; in more favourable seasons again the native hunters kill their five and six during the summer and autumn. The flesh of the wild camel, which is very fat in autumn, is used for food, and the skins for cloth-ing. These fetch ten tengas or a ruble and thirty copecks at Lob-nor.

The hunters of Lake Lob assured us that all the camels came from, and retired to, the Kum-tagh deserts. But these are entirely inaccessible, owing to the absence of water. At all events, none of the Lob-nortsi had ever been there. Some had made the attempt, starting from Chaglyk spring; but after struggling for a couple of days in loose sand-drift, where men and pack animals sank knee-deep, they became exhausted, and returned home unsuccessful. Total absence of water, however, there cannot be in the Kum-tagh; for if this were the case, camels could not live there; probably springs may be found which serve as drinking-places.   These animals, like their domesticated congeners, are not particular as to food, and can, therefore, safely inhabit the wildest and most barren desert, provided that they are far removed from man.

During the excessive heats in summer, the camels are attracted by the cool temperature of the higher valleys of Altyn-tagh, and make their way thither to an altitude of 11,000 feet, and even higher, for our guides informed us that they are occasionally found on the lofty plateau on its southern side.   Here the chief attraction for them are the springs of water, to say nothing of the greater abundance of camel's thorn (*calidium*), and their favourite, but less plentiful *Hedysarum*. In winter the wild camel keeps entirely to the lower and warmer desert, only entering the mountains from time to time.

Unlike the domesticated animal, whose chief characteristics are cowardice, stupidity, and apathy, the wild variety is remarkable for its sagacity and admirably developed senses.   Its sight is marvellously keen, hearing exceedingly acute, and sense of smell wonderfully perfect. The hunters told us that a camel could scent a man several versts off, see him, however cautiously he might approach, from a great distance, and hear the slightest rustle of his footsteps.   Once aware of its danger, it instantly takes to flight,

and never stops for some dozens, or even hundreds
of versts. A camel I fired at certainly ran twenty
versts without stopping, as I saw by its traces,
and probably farther still, had I been able to follow
it, for it turned into a ravine off our line of march.
One would suppose that so uncouth an animal
would be incapable of climbing mountains;
the contrary, however, is actually the case,
for we often saw the tracks and droppings of
camels in the narrowest gorges, and on slopes
steep enough to baffle the hunter. Here their
footprints are mingled with those of the mountain
sheep (*Pseudo Nahoor*) and the arkari (*Ovis Poli*).
So incredible did this appear, that we could hardly
believe our eyes when we saw it. The wild camel
is very swift, its pace being almost invariably a
trot. In this respect, however, the domesticated
species will, in a long distance, overtake a good
galloper. It is very weak when wounded, and
drops directly it is hit by a bullet of small calibre,
such as the hunters of Lob-nor use.

The wild camel pairs in winter, from the middle
of January nearly to the end of February. At
such times the old males collect troops of some
dozens of females, and jealously guard them
from the attentions of their rivals. They have
even been known to drive their wives into some
secluded glen, and keep them in it as long as
the rutting season lasts. At this period too frequent fights take place between the males, often
terminating in the death of one or other of the

combatants. An old male, when he has over-powered a younger and weaker antagonist, will crush his skull between his teeth.

Females bear once in three years, the period of gestation being rather over the year; the young camels are born, never more than one at a time, early in spring, i. e. in March. They are much attached to their dams. Should one of these latter be killed, the young camel takes to flight, returning, however, again later to the same spot. When caught young, wild camels are easily tamed and taught to carry a pack.

Their voice, very rarely heard, is a deep, lowing noise; in this way the dams call their young; males, even during the rutting season, utter no sound, but find their consorts by scent.

We were unable to learn the duration of a camel's life; some are known to live to a great age. Our hunter-guide once chanced to kill a he-camel, with teeth completely worn down, notwithstanding which the animal was in good condition.

The Lob-nortsi, who hunt the wild camel in summer and autumn, never go expressly in search of it, but kill them whenever they get the chance.

This sport is generally very difficult, and only three or four hunters in the whole district of Lob-nor engage in it. The ordinary mode of killing camels is by lying in wait for them at the watering-places, not by following on their fresh tracks. The hunters I sent out in search of this

animal did not return to Lob-nor before the 10th
March, but they were successful. On the border
of the Kum-tagh they killed a male and female,
and quite unexpectedly obtained a colt, by taking
it from its dead mother's womb. This young
camel would, in the natural course, have been
born on the following day.

The skins of all three specimens were excellent,
and had been prepared in the best way, by the
hunters, to whom we had given lessons in the art
of skinning and dressing. The skulls were also
perfect. Some days afterwards I received another
skin of a wild camel (male), killed on the Lower
Tarim. This specimen was a little inferior to the
others, because the animal from which it was
taken, came from a warmer climate, and had
already begun to shed its coat, besides having been
unscientifically skinned. I need scarcely say how
glad I was at length to procure the skin of an
animal about which Marco Polo had written, but
which no European had hitherto seen.[1]

From a zoological point of view there is little
to distinguish the wild from the domesticated
camel, and, as far as we could judge from a
superficial glance, the differences are the following,
viz. :—(a) there are no corns on the forelegs of
the wild specimen ; (b) the humps are half the

---

[1] [This is a mistake, Marco Polo makes no mention of the
wild camel. The earliest credible record we have of it is that of
Shah Rukh's envoys in 1420. See *Cathay*, &c., 1, cc., and introduction to Prejevalsky's *Mongolia*.—M., &c.]

size as compared with those of the tame breed,[*] and the long hair on the top of the humps is shorter; (c) the male has no crest, or a very small one; (d) the colour of all wild camels is the same—a reddish sandy hue; this is rare with domestic animals; (e) the muzzle is more grizzled, and apparently shorter; (f) the ears are also shorter. In addition to these peculiarities, wild camels are generally remarkable for their medium size; huge brutes such as are sometimes seen among their domestic brethren are never found in a wild state.

Now as to the question—are the camels found by us the direct descendants of wild parents, or are they domesticated specimens which have wandered into the steppe, become wild, and multiplied in a state of nature? Each of these questions can be answered both in the affirmative and negative. In South America we find an instance of domesticated animals running wild and multiplying, as where a few horned cattle and horses have escaped from the Spanish colonies and increased on the free pasture-lands into great herds. A similar instance, on a smaller scale, attracted my attention in Ordos, where, after the Dungan insurrection, in the course of some two

---

[*] The flesh of an eleven-year-old camel obtained for us from Tarim had not been removed, so that we could easily take the measurement. The result was that the humps of this full-grown male were only seven inches high, whilst those of domestic camels not unfrequently measure 1½ ft., and even more.

or three years cows and bulls had become as
wild and difficult to stalk as antelope.[3] But
with regard to the multiplying of camels which
had obtained their liberty, a difficulty arises in
the circumstance of there being very few males
of the domesticated kind fit for the stud, and
lastly, the acts of breeding and birth are for the
most part performed with the assistance of man.
Assuming that the latter of these difficulties may
disappear when leading a free life, the other
nevertheless remains, i. e. the irremediable injury
produced by castration. Few chances, therefore,
remain of camels capable of breeding escaping;
one exception must, however, be made in the case
of interbreeding of wild male with female domesticated camels.

On the other hand, the localities fit for human
habitation in the basin of Lob-nor are particularly
ill-suited for camels, owing to the damp climate,
insects, and bad food. Hence the population
could hardly at any time have kept many, and
now the Lob-nortsi keep none at all.[4]

Turning to the other proposition, i. e. that the
wild camel of the present day is directly descended
from wild ancestors, more weighty evidence may,
I think, be adduced in support of this theory. It

[3] [Cf. *Mongolia*, i. 212.]

[4] In other parts, however, of Eastern Turkestan there are
plenty of camels, and probably there were more in ancient
times, when the relations of this country with China were closer
than they are now.

is true that besides the peculiarities we have already enumerated, this animal in its wild state possesses those qualifications developed in the highest degree which should enable it in its struggle for life to have every chance of preserving itself and its young. The admirable development of its external senses saves it from enemies; moreover these are very few in number in the localities that it inhabits—man and wolves being the only ones it has to encounter. Even wolves are rare in the desert, and would scarcely be dangerous to a full-grown camel. Besides being habitually wary, it will resort to the most inaccessible spots to avoid man, and it is probable that the sandy wastes to the east of Lake Lob have served time out of mind as its settled abode. Of course in earlier ages the limits of its distribution may have extended much farther than at the present time, when all that remains for it is the most remote corner of the great desert of Central Asia.

On comparing the above-mentioned data, it seems to me possible to arrive at the conclusion that the wild camel of the present day is the direct descendant of wild parents, but that from time to time escaped domesticated animals probably became mixed with them. The latter, or rather such as were capable of begetting stock, left offspring, and these in after-ages could not be distinguished from wild camels. But in order to decide this point finally it will be of importance to compare the skulls of the two varieties.

In the first days of February we returned to Lob-nor, of which with the Lower Tarim we will now speak.

After uniting near Airilgan ferry with the Kiok-ala-daria, the Tarim, as we have already said, flows for about seventy versts nearly due south, and then falls into, or rather forms by its discharge, Lake Kara-buran. This name signifies "black storm," and has been given to the lake by the natives on account of the great waves which rise on its surface during a storm; and also because with a wind from the east or north-east (most frequent in spring) the Kara-buran inundates the salt marshes for a great distance towards the south-west, so much so as to interrupt for a time the communications between the Tarim and the village of Chargalyk.

Lake Kara-buran itself is from thirty to thirty-five versts long, and ten to twelve versts wide. Its area, however, depends a good deal upon the quantity of water in the Tarim; with high water the flat shores of the lake are flooded for some distance, whilst with low water the salt marshes on its borders are uncovered. Lake Kara-buran is not above three to four feet deep, and in places even less than this, although occasional deep pools occur, and the open space free from reeds is

H

comparatively larger than on Lob-nor. At the point where the Tarim flows into Kara-buran, another small stream, the Cherchen-daria, to which we have referred earlier, joins it from the west.

On issuing from Kara-buran the Tarim again appears as a river of some importance, but it soon rapidly diminishes, owing to the numerous canals by means of which the inhabitants draw off the water for fishing purposes. On the opposite bank the neighbouring desert continually encroaches upon the land capable of cultivation, scorching with its fiery breath every spare drop of moisture, and finally arresting the further progress of the river eastward. The struggle is over, the desert has gained the mastery over the river, life is swallowed up in death. But before finally disappearing, the Tarim forms by the overflow of its last waters an extensive reedy marsh known from ancient times as Lob-nor. The name Lob-nor as applied to the lake is unknown to the natives by whom the whole lower course of the Tarim receives this appellation, whilst the lake itself goes by the general name of Chon-kul (i. e. great lake) or more often Kara-kurchin, denoting the whole administrative district. In order to avoid confusion, I will continue to use the ancient name of Lob-nor.

This lake, or more strictly speaking this marsh, is in shape an irregular ellipse elongated from

S.W. to N.E., its maximum length in this direction being ninety to a hundred versts, whilst its width nowhere exceeds twenty. Such at least is the description that the inhabitants give of it. As for myself, I could only explore the southern and western shores, and accomplish a boat voyage down the Tarim to the centre of the lake; farther than this it was not possible to advance, owing to the thick reeds and shallows, indeed the whole of Lobnor is over-grown with reeds, leaving a belt of clear water. (from one to three versts wide) along the southern shore, and small open spaces studded like stars over the reedy expanse.

From the accounts given us by the natives it appears that the lake was clearer and deeper thirty years ago. Since that time the stream of the Tarim continually decreased, and the lake became shallower as the reeds multiplied. This went on for twenty years, but during the last six the volume of water has been again on the increase, and as the former lake bed, choked with reeds, is no longer large enough to contain it, the river now overflows its shores.

In this way not very long ago the belt of clear water extending along the whole southern shore of Lake Lob was formed. Beneath the surface may be seen the roots and stumps of tamarisk trees, which once grew on dry land. The depth is for the most part only two or three feet, rarely four or six feet, and for 300 or even 500 paces

from the shore barely exceeds one foot. The whole
of Lob-nor is equally shallow, only here and there
occur occasional pools, ten or at most twelve to
thirteen feet deep. The water in all parts of the lake
is clear and sweet, being brackish only round the
shores, which are salt and swampy, devoid of all
vegetation, and furrowed in ridges on the surface.
These saline marshes surround the whole of Lob-
nor; along the southern shore their width is from
eight to ten versts, whilst on the east, according
to the report of the inhabitants, they extend much
farther till they blend with the sands.   Beyond
the salt marshes, at all events on the south where
I surveyed them, a narrow belt of tamarisk-trees
follows the shore line, and beyond this again a
pebbly plain rising considerably though gradually
to the foot of Altyn-tagh.   This was probably in
remote times the border of Lake Lob itself, which
at that period overflowed its shores, and was therefore far more extensive, and probably deeper and
less obstructed by reeds than at present.   What
caused the diminution of the lake, and whether
this phenomenon was periodical or not, I cannot
say.   But the fact that almost all the lakes of Central Asia show signs of desiccation is well known.
Let us now say a few words about the Tarim.

At the western extremity of Lake Lob, near
the village of Abdallah, this river has still a width
of 125 feet, greatest mean depth fourteen feet,
velocity of current 170 feet per minute, sectional

area 1270 square feet, channel trough-shaped as before.

Below Abdallah the Tarim rapidly diminishes in size. Thus twenty versts lower its width is no more than fifty to fifty-six feet, and twenty versts lower still twenty to thirty feet, although its depth is from seven to ten feet, and the velocity of its stream considerable. For twenty versts farther the Tarim continues to flow as a brook of this kind, making several sharp bends, and at length entirely disappearing in the reeds. Farther to the north-east, and even before going so far, extend reedy and for the most part impassable marshes. It is impossible to cleave a passage even for the smallest canoe through this dense growth of canes, growing to a height of twenty feet and upwards in some places, and measuring one inch in the diameter of the stems. These monster canes fringe in one continuous alley the banks of the Tarim itself, whilst in shallower and more stagnant places grows water asparagus (*Hippuris*). Besides the canebrake we found all over Lob-nor cat's tail (*Typha*) and water-gladiole (*Butomus*); but of other water-plants, at least in early spring, there are none.

There is an abundance of fish in the lake of the same two kinds as in the Tarim, viz. marena (*Coregonus marœna*), and another of the carp family unknown to me. The first mentioned is by far the most plentiful in Lob-nor. The inhabitants call it *balik*, i. e. fish in general, and the other with a spotted back, the *tazek-balik*. Both kinds spawn in March.

The fishing begins in the early spring, and terminates late in the autumn. Small nets are used for this purpose in which the fish entangle themselves. The usual and most profitable method practised by the inhabitants may be described as follows :—a convenient spot having been selected for the purpose, a passage is cut into the Tarim (whose level, as we have already observed, is higher than the flats along-side it) water then pours out upon the plain, and a shallow but wide-spreading lake gradually forms, into which the fish find their way through the channel from the river. In May the opening is blocked up and the water ceases to flow. During the summer the great evaporation gra-dually dries up these artificial lakes, except in the deeper parts where the fish all congregate, and about the month of September the natives pro-ceed to take them; for this purpose a small aperture is again made, and a net placed there. The lake-fish, tired with their long confinement in the small pools, no sooner feel the rush of fresh water from the river than they hasten to meet it, and are caught in the trap. In this way the take is sometimes very large, and supplies are thus laid in for the winter. Moreover the inhabitants say that the long confinement in stagnant water impregnated with the salt of the soil makes the fish fat, and gives them a fine flavour.

As the banks of the Tarim upon entering the lake are flat, the dwellers on Lob-nor cannot employ the same method of ensuring food for the winter, but wherever it is possible they dig trenches between the river and the lakelets, and place nets there. Owing, however, to the vast quantity of fish, other modes of taking them are equally successful. We were told that Lob-nor freezes over in November,[*] and thaws early in March, the ice being from one to two feet thick.

In winter when frost drives southwards the innumerable water-fowl, animal life becomes very scarce. At such times the reeds are only tenanted by small flocks of the bearded titmouse (*Panurus barbatus*), *Cynchramus schœniclus*, and *C. pyrrhuloides*. Now and again a kite (*Circus rufus, C. cyanus*) wings its noiseless, stealthy flight overhead. In the salt marshes along the shore you may occasionally flush a covey of small larks (*Alaudula leucophœa?*); woodpeckers, *Rhodopophilus deserti*, and *Passer ammodendri* are sometimes found in the tamarisk bushes; black crows (*C. orientalis*) haunt the villages, and an occasional chough (*Podoces Biddulphii*) may be found on the drier ground. If to these be added

---

[*] Sometimes in the early part, sometimes not till the end of this month.

a few pheasants,[*] and wintering meadow-pipits, swans and bitterns, our list of the *avi-fauna* of Lob-nor will be complete.

The commonest forms of mammalia are the tiger, wolf, fox, wild boar, hare, and *djiran*, all in small numbers; of the lesser rodents, even such as sand-martens and mice, there are but very few.

In spring, however, especially at its commencement, Lob-nor is literally alive with water-fowl. Situated in the very midst of a wild and barren desert, half-way between north and south, it serves without doubt as an admirable resting-place for birds of passage, belonging to the web-footed and wading orders.

Were there no Tarim water-system, their flight would doubtless take a very different direction. But for this lake, they would find no resting-place between India and Siberia, and the winged travellers could never cross in one flight the whole distance from the Himalayas to the Tian-Shan.

Before proceeding to describe spring on Lobnor, let us say a few words about its inhabitants, the Kara-Kurchintsi, who inhabit eleven villages mostly situated in the midst of Lob-nor; of these the following is a list: Cheglik, six houses; Tuguz-ata, eleven; Abdallah, six; Kuchak-ata, two; Kum-chapkan, fifteen; Kum-luk, four;

---

[*] The same kind as on the Tarim and Kaidu-gol.

Uitun, five; Shakel, four; Kara-Kurchin, two
villages with four houses in each; besides these,
nine families are settled at Chargalyk. The
Kara-Kurchintsi therefore number some seventy
families, with a population of 300 souls of both
sexes.

The increase of population at Lob-nor is very
trifling, the reason of course being the unfavourable conditions of life there. Five or six children
in a family are rare, the usual number being two or
three, and sometimes there are none at all.

In earlier but not very remote times Lob-nor
was far more numerously populated than it is
now; it numbered then some 550 families, two-
thirds of whom lived on the lake itself, but
twenty years ago the small-pox destroyed in the
course of a few months nearly all the inhabitants, and most of those who survived had been
attacked by the disease. However, even these
insignificant remnants of the former people of
Lob-nor were only preserved in their primitive
state within the lake itself. The other inhabitants had already commenced an altered mode of
life; they kept flocks of sheep, and bred horned
cattle in small numbers, sowed corn and made bread
of it. This change for the better, at all events
in agriculture, began not very long ago under the
influence of the Khoten immigrants living at
Chargalyk, and it is in the neighbourhood of this
village that the native population sow their wheat

in the latter half of March, there being no land
suitable for the purpose at Lob-nor itself.[']

The favourable opportunity now afforded me of
seeing all that was left of the primitive life of the
inhabitants of Lob-nor,[*] was so much the more
valuable, as in the course of a decade or two what
I am now relating will seem like a tradition of
bygone times.

In appearance the inhabitants of Kara-Kur-
chinia and the Tarim present a strange mixture
of facial types, some of which call to mind the
Mongolian race.   The prevailing characteristics
are however Aryan, though far from pure. As
far as I could judge, the distinctive traits of a
native of these parts are height, rather below the
average ; frame, weak and hollow-chested ; cheek-
bones prominent, and chin pointed ; beard scanty
and à l'Espagnole ; whiskers even smaller ; hair on
the face generally of feeble growth ; lips often
thick and protruding ; teeth white and regular,
and skin dark, whence their name (Kara-Kurchin,
i. e. black Koshun) may be derived.

One language prevails among all the inhabitants
of this region.   It is said to resemble closely
the dialect of Khoten, but to be distinct from
that of Korla and Turfan.   The inhabitants on

['] Besides this a little corn is sown on some land on the
Djagansai-daria, near the site of a ruined town.

[*] About the middle of March, when the ice had finally
thawed, I visited all the Lob-nor villages in a boat.

the Tarim and Lob-nor are in general descended from a common stock, whilst those on the latter fell more under the influence and influx of foreigners from the oases at the foot of the Tian-Shan.

Now for a few words on the lake-dwellers of Lob-nor. And first about their habitations.

As the traveller descends the narrow, tortuous channel of the Tarim between rows of huge canes, he suddenly comes upon three or four boats moored to the river bank, and farther on a clear space on which, closely grouped together, stand some square, reed-made enclosures. This is a village. Its inhabitants, startled at the unusual sight of a stranger, have hidden themselves, and are taking a furtive look through their reed walls, but recognizing the rowers as their own people, and their chief among them, they come forward and assist in mooring the boats. You land and look around—nought to be seen but marsh and reeds, not a dry spot anywhere; wild duck and geese are paddling about close to the dwelling-place itself, and an old wild boar is quietly wallowing in the mud almost between the houses. So little does the native of these parts resemble a man, that even the shy wild animal fears him not!

Let us enter. Here is a square enclosure made of reeds, the only building material, for even the posts supporting the sides and corners of the enclosure are made of sheaves of them bound to-

gether. Reeds, too, are laid on the ground, and
serve as a slight covering to the marshy soil, so
that you are not obliged actually to sit in the
mud. I have seen in some huts the winter's ice
beneath this reedy flooring unthawed as late as
the middle of March. Each face of the dwelling-
place is twenty feet long; the entrance is from the
south. The roof is also made of reeds; but so
miserably put together that it does not even
shelter from the sun's rays, much less from the
bad weather; and the same with the walls, the
wind blows right through them during a storm as
easily as it does through the growing rushes.

In the middle of the floor a small hole is
scooped out for a fireplace; the fuel is also composed of reeds; indeed these are invaluable to the
inhabitants, supplying them with building materials
and fuel; the young spring shoots are used for
food, and the autumnal sweepings are gathered
for bedding. Lastly, these latter, when boiled
down, yield a dark, glutinous, and sweet substance, eaten by the natives instead of sugar.

Another plant of equal importance to the
inhabitants of Lob-nor and Tarim is the *asclepias*,
a shrub which, like our hemp plant, yields
a fibre from which yarn is spun and cloth prepared for wearing apparel, as well as nets for
fishing. The asclepias grows in abundance along
the whole course of the Lower Tarim, but there is
scarcely any on Lake Lob. Hence the natives

have to seek it on the Tarim in spring and autumn, preparing it in the manner we have described.

The garments made from the cloth, and worn by the natives, consist of a cloak and trousers; the winter head-dress is· a sheepskin cap, that in summer is of felt. The feet are uncovered, except in winter, and the shoes then worn are of the very poorest description, made of undressed hide; in summer even the head men go bare-footed. In winter the cloaks are lined with duck-skins dressed with salt, whilst the down and feathers are mixed with dry reeds and used for bedding. But this is luxury to the Kara-Kurchinian, many lie down to sleep on the bare rushes that litter the marshy floor, with nothing to cover them but the tattered cloak they wear during the day. For the sake of warmth these miserable creatures roll themselves up like balls, often on their backs, with hands and feet tucked under them. In this way five of our boatmen slept all huddled together, a living lump of humanity.

The food of the inhabitants consists chiefly of fish, fresh in summer, dried in winter. They boil the fresh fish, and drink the water in which it is boiled as we should tea; the dried fish is first steeped in salt water, and then fried. In neither case are the scales removed in the cooking pro-cess, this is done while they are being eaten. In

spring, and part of summer and autumn, ducks
trapped in nets form a variety to the fish-diet;
and as a particular treat in spring, they cook and
eat the tender young shoots of the reeds. They
eat neither bread nor mutton, owing to the scarcity
of both; whenever they obtain flour from Chargalyk, they roast it over the fire. Some of them
cannot even eat mutton, for it injuriously affects
their digestive organs, unaccustomed to such food.

In order to give an idea of the life these people
lead, I will enumerate the property belonging to
the family in whose house I passed several days
during a storm. It consisted of—two boats and
some nets outside; within the house, a cast-iron
bowl of Korla manufacture, an axe, two wooden
cups, a wooden dish, ladle and bucket made at
home of poplar wood; a knife and razor belonging
to the master of the house, a few needles, a loom
and distaff belonging to the mistress, the wearing
apparel of the whole family, two cloths made of
asclepias fibre, some strings of dried fish, *et voilà
tout.* The wrought-iron implements are from Chargalyk, and might serve as specimens of the iron
age, so rude is the workmanship. The axe had
not even an opening for the handle, which was
fastened to the bent edge of the head.[9]

The native of this country is as poor and
weak morally as he is physically. His thoughts
and ideas are limited by the narrow framework

* I have one of these axes in my collection.

of his surroundings, and he knows nothing beyond.   Boats, nets, fish, ducks, and reeds, these
are the only things step-mother nature has endowed
him with.   Under such circumstances, it may be
easily imagined how incapable he becomes of developing his faculties, excluded as he is from all
intercourse with an outer world.   He thinks of,
hopes for nothing beyond his native lake, the rest
of the world does not exist for him.   A constant
conflict with want, hunger, and cold has laid a
stamp of apathy and moroseness on his character.
He hardly ever laughs, nor do his thoughts soar
above the necessities of the present—fishing,
hunting, and the routine of his daily life.   Many
of these people are unable to count up to a
hundred; a few, however, of the more civilized
among them are artful and cunning in ordinary
transactions. The Mohammedan religion, although
professed by all, has not taken deep root among
them; I never once saw its rites and ceremonies
performed, and in the whole of Lob-nor there is
not one *akhoond*.   Prayers during circumcision,
marriage, and funerals are read aloud by the
educated son of the local governor, who is at such
times generally concealed from sight.

Circumcision is performed in the fourth or
fifth year, generally in the spring season, when
fish and ducks are plentiful enough to provide
entertainment for the neighbours. Girls marry
at the age of fourteen or fifteen; men at the

same age or a little over. The betrothal, however, is sometimes much earlier, often when the bride and bridegroom are not above ten years of age. The *Kalym* or purchase-money paid to the bride's parents is considerable—ten bundles of asclepias fibre, ten strings of dried fish, and a hundred or two of ducks. Immorality is severely punished; but the husband is allowed to turn his wife out of doors and take another. Upon the death of the husband the care of the wife devolves on the brother or some other near relative of the deceased. The lot of the women is more burdensome than that of the men. The wife is certainly mistress of her household, but how little is comprised in this word is evident from the fact that almost all the possessions are articles of daily use and consumption. During the husband's absence from home the wife mends the nets; upon her alone devolves the troublesome task of weaving the asclepias cloth, and she too assists the husband in collecting reeds for fuel and building purposes.

Externally the women are very unattractive; the old women are especially hideous, and one of those I saw at Lob-nor, emaciated, wrinkled, clad in rags, with matted hair, and shivering from ague, presented a most sorry likeness of humanity.[1]

---

[1] If I remember right, Darwin makes similar remarks on the *pécheresses* whom he met in a boat near the shores of Patagonia.

They bury their dead in boats—one serving
for the bottom, another for the lid of the coffin,
which is fixed on low supports in a slight hollow
dug in the ground; earth is then thrown over
the grave. Half the nets of the deceased are
buried with him [*] the remainder devolving on his
relatives. His boats and nets are generally the
most precious of the possessions of the Kara-
Kurchinian, for they afford him the means of
subsistence. The boats—or, more strictly speaking, the canoes—are from twelve to fourteen
feet in length by a foot and a half wide,
and even narrower. In this cockleshell the native
stands up; no matter how strong the wind,
navigating his craft as it dances over the waves
like a sea-bird. In calm weather and down
stream the swiftness of the boat rivals that of
the fish. The women are as expert in its management as the men: water is indeed their native
element.

Most of the fishing is done with small circular
nets, which are set in the narrow watercourses or
in channels specially dug for this purpose between
the lakes and the Tarim; these are examined
every morning and evening by their owners.
Long nets are, as an exception, set in the lakes,
and the fish are driven into them by beating the
water with the oars. When the take is successful
part of the booty is dried for winter use, when

[*] Nets are sometimes stretched round the grave.

fishing entirely ceases; but they continue to set
nets even after the first ice has formed.

The winter, although short in its duration,
is the most trying time for the wretched inhabitants, who suffer almost as much in their
reed habitations from the severe night frosts as
if they were exposed to the open air. It is certainly warm enough in the daytime; but then
another enemy—hunger—has to be encountered.
Well and good if the summer take has been large,
and stores laid by for future consumption. Some
years, however, the fishing is unsuccessful, and
winter brings with it starvation. In summer too it
is very little better. True, it is then warm and food
more plentiful. On the other hand, myriads of
flies and mosquitoes torment one the livelong day,
particularly in calm weather. These horrid insects appear about the middle of March, and do
not die off till late in the autumn. How the poor
children with their naked little bodies must suffer
when adults cannot rest comfortably at night for
them! The prevailing form of disease on Lake
Lob and the Tarim is inflammation of the eyes,
owing to the saline dust which continually fills
the air; sores on the legs and rheumatism are
also not uncommon.

Such is the life of the wretched inhabitants of
Lob-nor, unknown to and knowing nothing of the
rest of the world. As I sat in one of these damp
reedy enclosures, surrounded by the semi-nude

inhabitants of one of the villages, I could not help thinking how many generations of progress separated me from my neighbours, and what the genius of man has been to raise from such beings as these, whom our remote ancestors most probably resembled, the Europeans of the present day! The wild people of Lob-nor eyed me with stupid wonder. But I was not less interested in them than they in me. There was a singular attractiveness and originality about the whole scene, in the midst of the distant, unknown lake, surrounded by human beings who vividly recalled to mind man's primitive condition.

We passed the whole of February and two-thirds of March on the shore of Lob-nor, this being the sixth consecutive spring I had devoted to ornithological observations over the wide expanse of Eastern and Central Asia from Lake Hanka in Manchuria to Lob-nor in Eastern Turkestan.

After looking about us, we finally located ourselves on the bank of the Tarim exactly opposite the western margin of Lob-nor itself, one verst from the little village of Abdallah, where the ruler of Lob-nor, Kunchikan Beg,[3] resides. On either side of us stretched continuous marshes and lakes, making it a difficult matter to find dry ground for

---

[3] This title means "Beg of the rising sun." The father of Kunchikan was named Djagansai Beg, i. e. "Ruler of the universe." It would appear that human vanity has penetrated into the wildest desert.

our camp. But the situation was singularly favourable for ornithological purposes. Every new arrival could be at once observed, and our expectations of a great flight of birds were not disappointed. Hardly had we reached Lob-nor on the 3rd of February than we saw many which had probably arrived a few days before, the gull (*Larus brunneicephalus*) and swan (*Cygnus olor ?*). Of the latter, however, we only saw one specimen, and this may have been a wintering bird. About the 6th of the month we found widgeon (*Casarca rutila*), red-crested pochard (*Fuligula rufina*) and grey goose (*Anser cinereus*) the day after pintails (*Dafila acuta*), and white and grey herons (*Ardea alba, A. cinerea*), and on the 8th February the ducks began to arrive *en masse*, chiefly of two kinds, pintails and pochard. For days together they sped onwards always from the west-south-west, continuing their flight farther to the east, evidently in search of open water, of which there was as yet very little visible. Having gained the eastern extremity of Lob-nor, and found only desert, they turned back, and settled down amongst the numerous lakelets and open pools. But their favourite haunts were the flat mud-banks overgrown with low saline bushes, and of these there were many near our camp. Here every day, particularly towards evening, vast flocks of them would congregate, densely crowding large areas of ice; the noise they made on rising into the air was like a hurricane, and their appearance from a distance resembled a thick cloud. It would be no exaggeration to say that there would be as many as two, three, and perhaps four or even five thousand collected together. These followed one another in quick succession, to mention nothing of smaller companies whirling ceaselessly in every direction. Hardly a minute passed, and not single but many flocks of both local and migratory birds might be noticed. The latter could always be distinguished by their higher, more rapid, but at the same time more regular flight. Tens and hundreds of thousands, probably millions of birds appeared at Lob-nor during the fortnight, beginning on the 8th February, that the flight was at its height. What prodigious quantities of food must be necessary for such numbers! And why do these birds leave their winter quarters in the south for northern countries, where it is so cold and dreary? Is it that they have not sufficient space in those strange lands, and that this obliges them to hurry their departure in order to gain the less populous countries of the north, where the happy days of pairing, and the difficult ones of rearing their young must be passed. There every bird of passage has its home, to be abandoned only for a short time, and with return of spring to be revisited by the winged wanderers, as eager to hasten homewards as they are loth to leave in autumn when the flight is prolonged for some months.

The observations on the spring flight at Lob-nor afforded new proofs that birds of passage do not take the shortest meridional course, but prefer a more favourable, though more circuitous route. All the flocks without exception which appeared at Lob-nor came from W.S.W., occasionally from S.W. and W.; not a bird flew direct from the south, over the Altyn-tagh Mountains, thus proving that migratory birds, or at all events water-fowl, will not venture to cross the lofty and cold Tibetan highlands on their passage from the trans-Himalayan countries, but pass over this difficult country at its narrowest point.[4]

In all probability the feathered kind follow the Indian valleys to the neighbourhood of Khoten, and then take the direction of the Tarim and Lobnor across the warmer and less elevated districts. This explains the reason of their following a W.S.W. and not S. course to Lob-nor. And we were told by the inhabitants that in autumn they depart in the same direction.

As soon as the great flight of birds began in earnest our days were passed in sport. The

---

[4] [But there are doubtless lakes in Tibet fed by warm springs, resorted to by birds early in the year. Captain Trotter mentions having seen waterfowl at Wood's Victoria Lake on the great Pamir, where he detected the presence of warm springs. (See his report on the survey operations in E. Turkestan, p. 52 and passim.) And Sir D. Forsyth mentions having found stragglers of these birds frozen to death in their flight across the mountains in October (Report, p. 70).—M.]

Cossacks [5] also took an active part, making use of shot manufactured by themselves. Our supply of lead, however, was soon exhausted, and our companions were obliged to discontinue their pastime; the rifles I reserved for large birds, such as geese, swans, eagles, &c. Duck-shooting was always absurdly easy. We counted the slain by dozens, although we husbanded our ammunition, having only a small quantity, and no use for the ducks we killed. Of these we required three apiece for food, so that we boiled twenty-four ducks in our saucepan for breakfast, dinner, and supper daily. Such are travellers' appetites sharpened by out-door life and constant exercise—the best of antidotes against stomachic disorders and sleeplessness. We usually started for the chase about noon or a little earlier, when the sun was getting warm and the ducks were feeding among the reeds, as they are wont to be less shy at this time than at any other. Besides, in my frequent walks over the ice, which had begun to thaw rapidly on these lakes about the middle of February, I often chanced to fall through to the waist, and a bath of this kind, disagreeable enough on a warm day, was quite unbearable on a frosty morning, necessitating a speedy return to camp.

[5] The Cossacks left behind at Chargalyk joined us at Lob-nor; hither too came Zaman Beg, who had gone to Korla at the bidding of Yakub Beg during our absence.

The sport began at our very *yurta*. On looking round, we invariably noticed several flocks, some on the mud along the shores of the lake, others on the ice, this latter being preferred by the pintail duck, whereas the pochards and gadwalls (*Anas strepera*) like the open water. Closely huddled together, the flock always utter a low, muffled note, and the clatter of their bills whilst dabbling the mud for food could be heard some distance off. After considering which of the flocks to stalk, you start in that direction, at first walking as usual, then in a stooping attitude, and lastly crawling on all fours. Under cover of the reeds you approach to within a hundred paces or even nearer, your heart almost in your mouth in your eagerness. Before you, like liquid mud, a number of ducks are huddled together, nothing but moving heads and white necks to be distinguished in that shapeless mass. Drawing breath, you aim—one barrel at them sitting, another as they rise, and ten birds, at least, killed and wounded, strew the ice or shore. Many, badly hit, fly some distance before falling, but there is no time to look for these; they must be left as the prey of eagles, crows and kites, who watch the sportsman's movements from afar.

As soon as shots are fired the nearest flocks rise in the air with the noise of a whirlwind; but after circling for awhile, they again settle down, sometimes in the very spot from which they rose. In the meanwhile you pick up the slain, and the wounded, collect them all together in a heap among the rushes, and go off in quest of more victims, when the same thing repeats itself. Sometimes the birds are seated a considerable distance from the reeds, preventing your approach, and obliging you to fire at 150 paces. In this case you may by chance kill a few with the largest-sized shot; but only those fall that are hit in the head, neck, or wing.

Weary of this sport, my companion and I would station ourselves in order to shoot single birds flying over our heads. This was the best way of obtaining specimens for our collections, for the packs were mostly composed of pintails. We almost always posted ourselves among the reeds, so as to be under cover, firing only at choice birds, for they flew over in such numbers that it would have been impossible to reload in time had we fired at every one. Now and again geese, herons, gulls, and kites fell to our guns. Of course there were the usual number of misses in spring shooting, but we invariably made a good bag at the end of two or three hours.

The inhabitants of Lob-nor never shoot ducks, but set traps wherever they are in the habit of resorting. In this way every trapper secures his two hundred birds in the course of the spring.

The principal flight was over as quickly as it began. The whole mass of ducks arrived in two

weeks' time, so that there were only occasional
new-comers between the 20th and 22nd of
February. But large as was the quantity of ducks,
the variety was so small that by the 19th of the
month we had only counted twenty-seven kinds.[6]
Of all these only three appeared in very great
numbers : pintails, pochards, and gadwalls. The
pintails were the most numerous of all, and we
could scarcely move a step without seeing some.
The others continued to arrive in small numbers
up to the end of February. Towards the end of
this month, however, a good many grey geese,
cormorants, and widgeon (*Anas penelope*) visited
the lake, and by the 18th even coots were seen.
It is surprising that such a bad flyer as the coot
can traverse at this early season of the year the
cold deserts of Western Tibet.[7] Two days

---

[6] The following is the order of their arrival :—*Larus brunneicephalus, Cygnus olor ? Fuligula rufina, Casarca rutila,
Anser cinereus, Anas acuta, Ardea alba, Ardea cinerea, Fuligula ferina, Graculus carbo, Anser indicus, Budytes citreoloides ?
Turdus ruficollis, Anas penelope, Larus argentatus ? Fuligula
nyroca, Anas boschas, A. clangula, A. crecca, Tadorna cornuta,
Fuligula cristata, Anas strepera, Sterna caspia, Botaurus
stellaris, Anas clypeata, Totanus calidris, Fulica atra.*

[7] [Hume says that the highest ranges " oppose no invincible
obstacle to the periodical migration of even the tiniest and
most feebled-winged of our songsters. It is startling to think
of birds like the *Phylloscopi*, ill-adapted as they seem for
lengthened flights, and, when not migrating, rarely flying more
than a few yards at a time, yearly travelling from Yarkand to
Southern India and back again. How these butterfly-like mites
brave in safety the vast stretches of almost Arctic deserts—ab-

before this I heard the cry of a bittern—also awkward on the wing—but he may have been a wintering bird.

It might be supposed that such enormous flocks of the feathered tribe would have imparted life to Lake Lob, and thoroughly roused it from its winter's slumber. But strange to say, this great assemblage of birds created very little stir in these regions. True, the observer might detect movement and bustle near the water's edge—a very bazaar of birds, but the air resounded hardly at all with the joyous songs and notes that harbinger spring-tide in our country. The feathered visitants kept together in flocks, neither disporting nor enjoying themselves, as though they knew it to be only a temporary resting-place, and that a more difficult, more distant journey lay before them. Those songs and notes so welcome to lovers of nature were never heard at Lob-nor, even when the weather was fine and bright, and no genial warmth was ushered in by early spring. Seated on the ice, the flocks murmured to themselves, as though taking counsel together on their further flight northwards. Of the local birds, a small lark (*Alaudula leucophæa ?*) would occasionally

solutely devoid of vegetation, where the thermometer habitually varies 50° in twelve hours, and a breeze springing up sends the mercury down far below zero, and freezes men, horses, and even yaks, it is alleged, in a few hours, is verily a mystery." *Lahore to Yarkand*, pp. 160 *et seqq.*—M.]

burst forth into song, and even he proved but an indifferent master of the art.

The weather during February was tolerably warm. At noon the thermometer rose in the shade to 55° Fahr.; after sunset in the first half of the month it fell to 5° Fahr., in the latter half it never stood below 15° Fahr. The sky was generally overcast with light fleecy or feathery clouds, and the atmosphere charged with dust resembling fog or smoke raised by winds which were neither particularly frequent nor violent, although twice (on both occasions from the N.E.) they blew with the force of a gale. While the storm lasted the dust was borne along in clouds entirely obscuring the sun. Indoors it became dusk as twilight, objects upwards of a hundred paces off were undistinguishable, and respiration was difficult. The gale usually subsided rapidly, but for days afterwards a powdery mist was suspended in the air. As the wind rose the cold increased as it generally does in Central Asia. No atmospheric deposits fell, and the air was terribly dry.

The lower course of the Tarim opened on the 4th February, but ice remained on the lakes till the beginning of March, although it had lost its whiteness by the end of February, and hardly held together.

Scarcely had the lakes opened in the first week of March, than all the feathered visitors of Lob-nor took their departure together for the north.

In two or three days the number of ducks was
diminished by one half. For nights in succession
we heard the noise of the departing flocks. They
rarely started in the daytime, but at night they
sped onwards without turning to right or left.
By the 10th or 12th of March the chief exodus
was over; the birds had left Lob-nor as quickly
as they had come. Again the lake was deserted
by the bulk of its February visitants; but the few
that remained to nest now began living in a more
spring-like fashion. The call-notes of ducks and
geese, the shrieks of gulls, the booming cry of the
bittern, and the whistle of the coot were more
frequent. In the evenings the reeds resounded
with the crake of the water-rail. These were all;
no other songsters enlivened the dreary marshes
of Lob-nor.

During the whole of March the arrival of new
birds was very deficient both in variety and
numbers.[a] Vegetation, notwithstanding the warm
weather which had set in, slumbered as in winter.
Not till the very last days of March did the young
green shoots of the reeds begin to spring up and

---

[a] In the first half of this month there appeared *Grus cinerea,
Lanius isabellinus, Buteo vulgaris, Pelicanus crispus?, Anas
querquedula, Saxicola leucomela, Mergus merganser, Podiceps
minor, Ægialites cantianus.* In the latter half of March arrived
*Sturnus vulgaris? Cypselus murarius, Sylvia curruca? Nu-
menius arquatus, Milvus ater, Saxicola atrigularis, Hirundo
rustica, Ciconia nigra, Cyanecula cœrulecula, and Hypsibates
himantopus.*

flower buds to darken the poplars. The cause of
the lateness of the vegetation was the terrible
dryness of the air and the periodical cold weather
both by night and day during the continuance of
the gales, which always blew from the N.E., and
occurred much oftener than in February. The
clouds of dust raised by these winds settled in
a thick layer on the reeds and bushes, rendering
it impossible to move a step without getting one's
eyes filled, and the sun shone luridly as through
smoke. There was not a single clear day all
through March and the first half of April. The
twilight both morning and evening lasted much
longer than usual, and the air was thick and heavy
to breathe.

We passed the end of March and two-thirds of
April in the valley of the Lower Tarim, on the way
from Lob-nor to the Tian-Shan. Of this well-
wooded country we had raised our expectations
too high. Here also the absence of spring life
was very marked. Notwithstanding the continual
and great heats up to 93° Fahr.[9] in the shade,
during April, it was not till the middle of this
month that the leaves of the poplar began to unfold,
and even then only partially.

The other bushes and the reeds on the marshes
still bore their yellowish wintry tint. Not a
flower nor butterfly could be seen ; in their stead

[9] [This must surely be a mistake; the heat in Persia in the
middle of August is hardly above 85° in the shade.—M.]

clouds of flies and mosquitoes thronged the marshes, and scorpions and tarantulas glided over the dry ground. The neighbouring desert was deprived even of these ornaments, neither lizard nor insect nor any living creature could be seen, nothing stirred the parching sand save the frequent whirlwinds riding like demons before the eyes of the traveller.

It became only a little more cheerful nearer the lakes, where blue-throated warblers and reed birds sang among the canebrake, and pheasants challenged. In the woods very few birds could be seen besides nesting starlings, sand-swallows, and shrikes. Of the smaller migratory birds there were none besides the wren. They all avoid the deserts of Lob-nor, and direct their flight by a neighbouring route to the forests of Siberia.

By the 10th of April the spring flight of birds in these regions was at an end. On the 19th of that month not far from the Tian-Shan we heard for the first time the note of the cuckoo, betokening the proximity of regions incomparably superior as regards climate and nature to the deserts in the midst of which we had passed nearly half a year.

Returning to Korla on the 25th of April, we were lodged in our former quarters, again shut up and placed under surveillance. On the fifth day after our arrival we had an interview with the then ruler of Eastern Turkestan, Yakub Beg, lately deceased. He received us graciously, or at all events appeared to do so, and while the audience lasted for about an hour continually assured us of his good-feeling towards Russians in general and towards me individually in particular. Facts, however, proved the contrary. A few days after the interview we were conducted to the Kaidu-gol, guarded as before, and, on taking leave of us, our escort had the impudence to demand a written document expressing our satisfaction at the way we had been treated during our stay in Djety-shar.[1]

In return for the presents we made Yakub Beg and his suite, we received four horses and ten camels [2]—the latter were all bad, and died two days after, thereby embarrassing us not a little when we entered the Balgantai-gol. It was no use to think of returning, yet we had only ten camels [3] and six horses left; so transferring the packs to the latter, and setting fire to all superfluous baggage, we marched on foot to Yulduz. Hence I despatched a Cossack and interpreter

---

[1] [Djety-shahr, i. e. the seven cities—a name given to Dzungaria, or Eastern Turkestan, after the seven important cities of Kashgar, Yarkand, Aksu, Khoten, Utch, Kucha, and Karashahr. —M.]

[2] Before this, on our way to Lob-nor, we received seven camels.

[3] Altogether, during the expedition to Lob-nor, from the time we left Kulja to our return thither, we lost thirty-two camels by death.

to Kulja, to give tidings of our difficult situation, and to ask for assistance. At the end of three weeks fresh pack-camels and supplies arrived in time to relieve our most urgent wants and revictual our empty commissariat, the stores taken from Korla having been soon exhausted, and the game we shot having been our only means of subsistence.

Arriving in Yulduz in the middle of May, we found vegetation very backward. The sun had not yet thawed the deep snow, or warmed the frozen ground,[4] and "winter lingering, chilled the lap of May." Even in the beginning of June the powers of light and darkness, Ahriman and Ormuz, still strove for the mastery. Night frosts, cold westerly and north-westerly winds, even snow[5] at times retarded the early vegetation. But the herbs and flowers of these regions are accustomed to such drawbacks. Give them a few hours' warmth in the daytime, and these children of spring will not long delay in developing their short-lived existence.

It is always thus in the mountains, and in those of Asia in particular. Hardly had one

---

[4] In winter snow is said to fall two to four feet thick ; on the hills it is even deeper than this. The frosts are very severe. In the middle of May we found on the Horeti-gol, at an elevation of 8500 feet above the sea, large sheets of ice two to three feet thick.

[5] In the latter end of May snow of considerable depth fell in the mountains up to an elevation of 9000 ft. above the sea.

K

passed through half of May, than with each suc-
ceeding day new kinds of flowers showed themselves. On all the moist mountain slopes and in the
valleys the wild garlic and the low-growing aconite
showed their yellow heads ; and, in smaller quantities, Pedicularis and violets began to appear. On
the drier ground the blue heads of the Pasque
flower (*Pulsatilla*) dotted the surface, and little
pink primroses lay scattered over the sides of the
hills. Somewhat later, on the dry, stony slopes,
saxifrage came into bloom, and last of all, the low,
prickly camel's thorn.

In the valleys and by the mountain springs,
wherever the sun's rays were hottest by the end
of May, appeared forget-me-nots, sun-dew, lady's
bed-straw, white and yellow dandelion, wild pea,
cinquefoil, stitchwort, and others.

The vegetation of the Yulduz plain is not
luxuriant, although its grass is mostly fit for
cattle. Flowers only adorned the damper ground
by the banks of streams, and this not in abundance. Besides two kinds of vetches, here and there
bloomed the blue iris and *cuckoo's tears*,⁶ whilst the
dry, clayey ground was studded with the tiny white
blossoms of the stonecrop. These complete the
list. The lakes and marshes on the Baga-Yulduz-
gol were worse off still, for here grew no flower-
ing plants of any kind. Animal life was more

---

* [The Russians give the name of " Cuckoo's tears " to the
spotted orchis *(orchis maculata).*—M.]

abundant in Yulduz in spring than we had found it in the preceding autumn. The animals were the same, but the marmots had now awakened from their winter's sleep, and their shrill whistle was unceasingly heard in the higher valleys. The increase in the numbers of birds was even more remarkable, especially of the smaller kinds, which here, as everywhere else, greeted spring with their cheerful melody. Among the stern cliffs of the alpine zone, the lively notes of the hedge-sparrow (*Accentor altaicus*) mingled now with the cluck and call of the partridge (*Megaloperdix nigellii ?*); here too mountain swallows (*Chelidon lagopoda*), and flocks of grey-headed finch, still unpaired, disported themselves; and the occasional note of a red-winged wall-creeper might be heard. Lower in the forest belt mountain finch and rock pipit were frequently met with; wagtail (*Budytes citreoleus*) and *Actitis hypaoleucos* nested near the streams, and ruddy sheldrake (*Casarca rutila*) and *Anser indicus* among the rocks. Still lower, at the entrances to the valleys, and on the plain, were field larks, and the stone chat (*Saxicola isabellina*), an exquisite songster. Ducks, storks, sandpipers, gulls and terns were building their nests on the marshes and lakes.

Insects were not numerous in the month of May, humble-bees being the commonest in the alpine meadows. Flies and mosquitoes cannot

K 2

exist on chilly Yulduz; of snakes and lizards there
are none, and only an occasional toad or frog may
be caught near a marshy spring.

Early in June we crossed the Narat range, on
the southern slopes of which the spring flora was
more abundant than in Yulduz, and descended to
the headwaters of the Tsanma.   Here the climate
and vegetation bore a totally different aspect:
forests of spruce fir and thick grass two feet
high clothed the valley and slopes of the mountains.   Rain fell daily; the rich black soil was
saturated with moisture like a sponge, and we
found the same humidity in the neighbouring
valley of the Kunges, only that in the latter,
owing to its lower elevation, vegetation was even
more advanced, and flowers more profuse.

Our herbarium received considerable accessions.
On the other hand, contrary to our expectations,
comparatively few nesting birds were found either
on the Tsanma or Kunges, the cause probably
being the extremely wild nature of the country,
avoided by small birds [7] in particular.   Now, too,
clouds of gnats and flies made their appearance,
from which there was no escape day or night.

[7] The most common on the Tsanma were *Carpodacus erythri-
nus, Sylvia superciliosa, Cuculus canorus, Scolopax rusticola,*
and *Turdus viscivorus* in the forests; *Crex pratensis, Sylvia
cinerea, Salicaria sphenura? Pratincola indica* in the meadow-
land.   On the Kunges, besides those we have mentioned, must
be added *Scops zorca, Oriolus galbula, Columba œnas, Columba
sp., Columba palumbus, Salicaria locustella,* and others.

On our excursions these horrible insects annoyed us mercilessly, and the sudden change of climate from dry and cold to damp and warmth, affected our health unfavourably, particularly on first arriving on the Kunges.

Having completed our researches here, we hastened to Kulja, where we arrived in the beginning of July, tired and ragged, but with a rich store of scientific booty.

On looking back, I could not but feel that fortune had again favoured me wonderfully. In all probability had we started a year earlier, or a year later, our exploration of Lob-nor would have been unsuccessful; for had it been earlier, Yakub Beg, who was then neither afraid of the Chinese, nor solicitous for the friendship of Russia, would hardly have allowed us to pass beyond the Tian Shan; whereas, had it been postponed until now, the journey would not have been possible, owing to the disturbed state of affairs consequent on the death of Yakub Beg.

REMARKS ON THE RESULTS OF COL. PREJE-VALSKY'S JOURNEY TO LOB-NOR AND ALTYN-TAGH, BY BARON VON RICHTHOFEN.

SIX centuries ago Marco Polo told his countrymen in Venice of the terrors of the desert of Lop. It was the first time that the European world heard of it. From Khoten the great traveller journeyed viâ Pein and Ciarcian, whose true situation was first quite recently indicated by the discernment of Colonel Yule. The road led him through deserts, in the midst of which those thinly populated places lay like oases at great intervals. In this way he reached the town of Lop. But a worse country yet remained for him to traverse. " Lop," says he, " is a large town at the edge of the Desert, which is called the Desert of Lop, and is situated between east and north-east. It belongs to the Great Khan, and the people worship Mahomet. Now such persons as propose to cross the Desert take a week's rest in this town to refresh themselves and their cattle ; and then they make ready for the journey, taking with them a month's supply for man and beast. On quitting the city they enter the Desert." For thirty days the Venetian journeyed through the land of drift-sand. He depicts in lifelike colours its terrors, its trackless wastes and its barrenness, which render it impossible to find the way except by the bleached bones of fallen men and animals. He also speaks of the strange sounds which travellers hear in the night ; these are the voices of ghosts and goblins who seek to lure him to ruin.

Ever since that time the " desert of Lop " has continued to occupy a place in the maps of Asia. Its position, however, was quite unknown for some centuries; for no European traveller that we know of followed the Venetian into these remote regions. In a roundabout way, however, during the last century the name Lop or Lob took a more definite shape. The Jesuits were wonderfully near the truth in their map of Central Asia probably constructed from native sources of information, and published by D'Anville in 1785 in Du Halde's great work. For the first time Lob-nor appears in it as a reservoir without an outlet, in which the rivers of Yarkand, Kashgar, and Karashahr terminate. It is placed S.E. of Turfan, in 91½° E. of Greenwich, and in 42½ N. Lat. An important correction was made by the Fathers D'Arocha, Espinha, and Hallerstein, who were sent by Kien-long to prepare a map of the districts belonging to his empire as far as the Pamir and beyond the Ili. They fixed astronomically the positions of a number of places, and compiled the remainder partly from itineraries and partly from Chinese maps.

At the same time many references to Lake Lob, and the historical importance of the adjacent country were found in Chinese literature. De Guignes was the first to collect them in his great work, " The History of the Huns." Soon afterwards some extraordinary views of the geographical importance of the lake sprung up. The Chinese could not understand how such a continual influx of water from so large a number of important streams could terminate so suddenly, and thought that they must take a further course and burst forth again elsewhere; and a remarkable combination of circumstances enabled them to fix the place where this was supposed to occur. It was a time-honoured tradition that the Yellow River rose in the Kuen-lun mountains. But at the time when geography received an impulse during the the Han dynasty (207 B.C.—221 A.D.) this range was unknown, and the Yellow River had not been traced to its source. When, therefore, General Chang-kien, on his return from his expedition to the west (127 B.C.) reported that he had rediscovered the Kuen-lun of the ancients to the south of Yu-tien (Khoten), the startling assertion, notwithstanding its boldness, was eagerly accepted. The waters flowing thence must, by not less bold a conclusion, be the origin of the Yellow

River. They were certainly seen to end in Lake Lob, but it was self-evident that they only dived under the earth and reappeared elsewhere as the Yellow River in an unexplored mountain region.

Afterwards the sources of this river were found in *Sing-su-hai* or the starry sea, about 500 geographical miles from Lake Lob, and about 10,000 feet higher.[1] But the old doctrine remained unshaken, and even at the present day the Chinese repeat the same theory in their Hsi-yu-ki, i. e. description of western lands,[2] where it is stated: "To the east and south-east of Lop-noor, one may see along the roads leading thither either naked steppes and marshland or mountains rising abruptly with snow-clad peaks, desert plains, and rivers. Innumerable springs start from their sides, and these, when viewed from a height, resemble a sea of stars. They are deep and burst out with great force; it is manifest that a mighty river flows underground. On the east are sand-hills, and on the south-east a sandy-steppe extending for 1000 li." The Yellow River, too, rises in a wide steppe basin where the numerous lakes have gained for it the name of "starry sea."

Klaproth's remarkable works first attached their full value to the surveys of the Jesuits in Kien-long's time, and made known in Europe all the geographical results derived from the native works. His map of Central Asia, which appeared in 1830, was particularly useful, and served Humboldt and Ritter for their work. The former deduced in a surprising way the probable elevation above sea-level of several places and assigned 200 *toises* as that of Lob-nor. Its geographical position was placed 3° farther west and about 2° farther south than D'Anville had fixed it (viz. 88½° long. east of Greenwich and 40¾° north lat. at the place where the Tarim flows into it). With but little variation these views held their ground, but the conclusive solution of all questions appeared to be very distant; for Lob-nor lay exactly in the centre of an extensive

[1] [Cf. *Mongolia*, ii. 180.—M.]
[2] From the *Hsi-yu-wonn Kien lu* (i. e. Guide to what one hears of Western lands and sees there) compiled in 1773, after a translation kindly made for me by Herr Himly.

region of Asia entirely beyond the reach of the European explorer.

Slowly were the barriers from the west broken through. After the year 1857, when Russian explorers began to investigate the Western Tian-Shan and its river system, Johnson in 1866 accomplished his important journey to Ilchi, the capital of Khoten; Hayward and Shaw soon followed, and reached Kashgar. Other English travellers have completed our knowledge of the tributaries which the Tarim receives from the west and south-west. It became manifest that the region which gives birth to this river is on a scale of grandeur such as no other river in the world can boast. It is girt round by a wide semicircular collar of mountains of the loftiest and grandest character, often rising in ridges of 18,000 to 20,000 feet in height, whilst the peaks shoot up to 25,000 and even 28,000 feet. The basin which fills in the horse-shoe-shaped space encompassed by these gigantic elevations, though deeply depressed below them, stands at a height above the sea varying from 6000 feet at the margin to about 2000 in the middle, and formed the bed of an ancient sea. From its wall-like sides on the south, west, and north, the waters rush headlong down, and though the winds, blowing from all directions deposit most of their moisture on the remoter sides of the surrounding ranges, viz. the southern foot of the Himalayas, the west side of the Pamir, and the northern slope of the Tian-Shan, the streams formed thereby winding through the cloud-capped, lofty cradle-land, and breaking through the mountain chains, reach the old ocean-bed only partly well-watered. The smallest of them disappear in the sand, others flow some distance before expanding into a level salt basin and there are absorbed. Only the largest, whose number the Chinese estimate at sixty, unite with the Tarim, a river 1150 miles long, and therefore in length between the Rhine and the Danube, but far surpassing both in the massiveness of surrounding mountains just as it exceeds the Danube in the extent of its basin. Its tributaries form along the foot of the mountains a number of fruitful oases, and these by means of artificial irrigation have been converted into flourishing, cultivated states, and have played an important part in the history of these regions.

As the westernmost of them from Keria and Khoten to
Kashgar became known through the above-mentioned explorations of Englishmen, the interest in the discovery of the
lake in which all these waters came to an end increased, a
knowledge of it appeared to be the necessary complement to
that of the whole of Eastern Turkestan. Hence the inquiries
made by travellers from the west had a particular object.
Some of these latter have compiled itineraries by means of which
the positions of places mentioned by Marco Polo on the way to
Lob-nor were in part determined.

The testimony of eye-witnesses acquainted us with the
existence of a place called Lob as well as a lake of that name
containing a great many fish. But many points of the problem
remained doubtful, amongst these was the geographical position
of the lake, although it could be gathered approximately from
the number of days' journey which it took to reach it by
various routes.

Shaw allowed too little for the day's journey and far too
much for the windings of the road, and so arrived at the conclusion that the lake must lie 4½ to 5 degrees of longitude
more to the west than its position on our maps.[1] Yule almost
on a similar basis reduced the western displacement to 3°,
whilst to others it seemed doubtful, partly on account of these
uncertain elements of calculation, and partly because of the
credibility of the authorities upon which the maps of the
Jesuits were based. The relative configuration of the ground
was another uncertainty. The elevation above sea-level of the
lake might be assumed to be probably about 2000 feet, but
opinions widely differed as to the character of the surrounding
country. Till within a few months ago the prevailing opinion
led one to suppose that the lake lay in an immense basin and
farther removed from its southern rampart than from that on
the north. Without a sufficient regard for Chinese sources of
information, nearly all existing maps gave the diameter of the

[1] Shaw reckoned the day's journey at twenty miles (Proc. R. G. S.
xvi. p. 243) and deducted about one-third for windings, making the net
amount covered per diem at thirteen miles (eleven and a half geographical
miles), whereas twenty-one geographical miles or seventy Chinese li and
one-seventh for windings is a truer allowance, making the distance per
diem eighteen geographical miles.

basin from north to south at about 880 geographical miles. On the other hand the accompanying map,[4] compiled from Chinese information, advances the mountainous country south of Lob-nor to beyond the 39th parallel, and reduces the width of the open basin in 88° long. to about 100 geographical miles.

Prejevalsky then had to settle questions of considerable interest. He had been attracted to the subject on his journey in Tsaidam when he had crossed a river, by following which up stream one would arrive at a country where the wild camel still existed, and reach Lob-nor without difficulty. He therefore determined to devote his next expedition to the solution of the geographical and zoological questions here awaiting him.

His accomplishment of this journey of which we now possess a detailed account, is one of the most important geographical feats of modern times. Taking his discoveries one by one, I shall often have to refer in the course of my remarks to the Chinese map. This is the well-known great map of China and Central Asia which appeared in the year 1862 in Wu-chang-fu, whilst for the rendering of the names I am indebted to Herr Carl Himly, whose extensive knowledge of languages enabled me to interpret the meaning of many of them.

1. *Little Yulduz Plateau.*—From Chinese maps and records, it appears that the Tian-Shan system is divided into parallel chains running from W. by S. and E. by N., by two plateaux, having a direction of W.N.W. and E.S.E., and known as the little and great Yulduz plateaux (*Kutshuk Yulduz* and *Angba Yulduz*). It was also known that along the first of these lay a road formerly much frequented, and that it was covered with rich pasturage. It appears to have been inhabited by a pastoral people, who were easily annihilated or expelled by invading hosts, so that at times the pasture-grounds were entirely deserted. In the fifteenth century the embassy sent by Shah Rukh, the son of Timur, to the court of China, took their outward journey through Yulduz, and the physician of the embassy has left us a description of the scenery. The Chinese often mention both of these high valleys, and inform us that *Yulduz*

----

[4] [An engraving of this map, from a tracing kindly sent me by Baron Richthofen, accompanies this volume.—M.]

signifies " Star." Prejevalsky confirms generally earlier information and gives us a very complete picture of the nature of this
high valley. From the valley of the Kunges, which he followed up
to a height of 4000 feet above the sea, he crossed, by a pass 6000
feet high, to the equally elevated valley of the Tsanma, which to
the south was shut in by the Narat, a mountain chain of alpine
character. A moderately steep ascent led him to the summit
of the Narat pass, 9800 feet high, whence he very gradually
descended to the lower end of Lesser Yulduz, 7000 to 8000 feet
above sea-level, which was deserted, owing to the Dungan war,
although eleven years ago the Turgutes, numbering 10,000
kebitkas, had nomadized here. A lofty range rising above the
snow-line, running from W.N.W. to E.S.E., divides Lesser from
Greater Yulduz. On the northern side the system of parallel
ranges to the Tian-Shan appears to set in. A road lies hence
to Urumtsi, and, according to Chinese maps, seems to cross the
principal chain of the Tengri-ula, by the pass of *Ulan-sadak-
dabaghan*. On the north, where Prejevalsky places a chain,
Odonkure, the Chinese map has a pass of a similar name, the
Odonghur-dabaghan. The inhabitants appear to be acquainted
with the names of the passes to the south, as the four names
given by Prejevalsky are coupled with the word *daban*. To
the east, according to the Chinese map, two passes lead from
the plateau, the *Habshil-dabaghan*, or " ravine pass," and the
Dalan-dabaghan, or " seventy passes." Judging from the
position and description, Prejevalsky's route lay over the
former, the height of which is set down at 9800 feet. The
ascent was gentle, the descent led through steep, rocky ravines.
The gorge of the *Habtsagai-gol* is forty versts long, and
probably answers to the *Khabtshil-ghool* of the Chinese map.
It is followed by that of the *Balgantai-gol*, twenty-two versts
long, and this brought the traveller to the *Kaidu*, at a height
of 3400 feet above sea-level.

The slopes on the southern side, unlike those on the north, are
bereft of all vegetation. "The neighbouring desert," says
Prejevalsky, "affixes the seal of death on this side of the Tian-
Shan, and the last drops of moisture are wrung out by the
snowy mountains of Yulduz."

2. *The Kurugh-tagh range.*—Without visiting the town of Karashahr and the great lake, Bostang-nor,[5] in its vicinity, into which the Kaidu-gol empties, the traveller turned southward, and here fell in with "the arid and sterile Kurugh-tagh range, of no great elevation." Till now it was marked on our maps as the *Kurunglo-tak*, a name derived from the town of *Korla* or *Kurungle*, situated on its southern side, towards which the route lay. The Kaidu-gol, shortly after leaving the lake, forces its way through the chain "by an exceedingly narrow ravine, ten versts long." The Chinese MSS. have described it in their favourite romantic way of expressing themselves. I borrow from one of them[6] the following extract :—

"The river flows for 100 li in a south-westerly direction, turns and flows south, through the mountains, and for a short distance beyond them, and then turns to the west. Here it flows past some old coal-mines, opened in 1815 by the Governor Yung-kung-kiu, continuing a little way further west, about half a li to the south of *Kalghi-aman-kintai*."

This is one of the forts described by Prejevalsky. "The river now enters the narrow, inhospitable gorge," which is depicted in very gloomy and picturesque language by the Chinese author. This important ravine in the history of the Chinese conquerors bore for a time the name of *Tie-men-kwan*, i. e. "Pass of the iron gate." On the south side stands another clay-built fort. Soon afterwards the town of Korla is reached, which our traveller was obliged to go round. According to Chinese reports it lies 150 li S.W. of Karashahr, and has a population of 700 families. The inhabitants are described as lazy, idle, quarrelsome, and unpolished. The products of the region are rice, corn, grapes, melons, and fruit, besides fish, crawfish, wild geese, ducks, herons, &c.

These explorations throw light on the strategical importance of the Kurugh-tagh pass, and on an episode of Chinese history. Immediately N.E. of Kalgha-aman, and probably a little

---

[5] Prejevalsky calls it *Bagarash*, the name in the text being taken from the Chinese map.

[6] *Hsi-yu-shui-tau-ki* (i. e. inventory of the water streams of the Western lands). It seems to have been compiled in the year 1821 by Hsu-sung.

on one side of our traveller's road, the Chinese map gives "Ruins of an old town." Here stood, as we learn from an old source of information, the ancient *Ului-chong*, which at the time of the Han dynasty was the seat of the Governor-General of the lands of Hsi-yu, i. e. for the whole of Eastern, sometimes too for Western Turkestan, and the whole country as far as the Caspian Sea. The distances of all places on the West, mentioned in the Han annals, are computed from Ului, as the most important place. We now see, after Prejevalsky has acquainted us with the physical character of those regions, that this was the most suitable place to afford military protection to the caravan roads south of Lob-nor, from the plundering and unruly tribes on the southern slope of the Tian-Shan.

3. *Character of the desert.*—Along the southern slope of the Kurugh-tagh lies a belt of country, twenty to twenty-five versts wide, covered with pebble and gravel. Prejevalsky assumed it to be the shore of a former sea. Beyond it lies "the boundless plain of the Tarim or Lob-nor desert," having a twofold character, i. e. consisting of a thin loam impregnated with salt on the west and of drift-sand on the east.

4. These points, however, do not call for any remarks, but with regard to the *river system* the map south of Korla assumes an entirely new aspect. Only the great western bend of the Kaidu, which Prejevalsky here calls the *Koncheh-daria*, was hitherto known, and perhaps as a more important river than it is now represented. This river does not, however, at present reach the Tarim, as the Chinese maps show $\frac{1}{4}°$ south of Korla, but after turning again to the east, directs its course far away from it before entering the intricate network of the Tarim channels. Whilst Korla has to be moved only 5' farther north and 8' farther west, than hitherto supposed, other positions have to be considerably altered, and Lob-nor should be placed contrary to Shaw's argument considerably to the south-east. The hydrography, as far as Prejevalsky learnt it, is shown on his map; but I will presently return to the question, whether it be probable that he has represented the whole river system.

5. *The Altyn-tagh Mountains.*—This is the most surprising of the discoveries of Prejevalsky, for it was generally supposed that there was an extensive tract of low country continuing through several degrees of Latitude to the south of the lake. But we now learn of a lofty range rising almost abruptly from the deepest part of the depression, visible at a distance of 150 versts, and on nearer approach taking the form of a gigantic wall (*vide supra*, p. 80). The discovery of this range is important both for geography and for the history of Central Asian intercourse. We can now understand why the old silk traders in their route to the western countries passed so close to the south of Lob-nor, although the dreadful desert lay between Sha-chau and the lake, for to the south the passage was blocked by mountains ; a road lay in that direction as well, but it was probably little used on account of the difficulties it presented. It is clear armies and trade caravans always marched through the kingdom of Leu-lan or Shen-shen, on the south shore of the lake. A new light too is now thrown on several passages of ancient history which were hitherto obscure. When the Chinese first turned their attention to the west, during the Han dynasty, Chang-kien, on his return in 127 B.C., from his remarkable expedition to Ferghana and the Oxus lands, found the whole country as far as 'the salt lake,' i. e. Lob-nor, occupied by the Huns, whose territory at that time covered wide tracts of Mongolia. He therefore endeavoured on his return to make a way through the territory which to the south joins the Tibetan province of *Kiang*, so as to avoid again falling into the hands of the Huns as he had done on the way out. Shortly after, in the years 121 and 119 B.C., Chinese troops under the command of the youthful General Ho-kiu-ping penetrated for the first time into the regions to the west, and found the right wing of the Huns settled on the salt lake and the Ping-nan Mountains (i. e. the mountainous region south of the plain). This was incomprehensible as long as extensive plains were believed to lie to the south of the lake ; whereas it is now evident that the Altyn-tagh opposed a natural barrier to their further advance, and that owing to their position at the foot of this range they must have completely controlled communications with the

west for armies and trade caravans. Similar considerations are suggested by the later Chinese wars with Central Asia.

6. *Lob-nor.*—It is remarkable that Prejevalsky found the last reservoir of the Tarim much farther south than the maps and Chinese information placed it, and that the water was fresh instead of salt. The Tarim discharges, according to the representation, in 39¼° N. Lat. and 89° E. Long., into a lake named Kara-buran, but again issues from its farther end, and forms a second lake, the Chon-kul or Kara-koshun. [Vide page 98.]

The first lake (Kara-buran) is, according to his description, only a preliminary basin, whose water must be the same as that in the river, and only undergoes change in summer, owing to evaporation. But the statement about the second basin, which answers to the true Lob-nor, and must be the last evaporating reservoir of the Tarim, is most surprising. The region through which the Tarim flows is highly charged with salt, springs of sweet water are rare, and only appear on the borders of the mountains; even in the high mountains the basins mostly contain salt, and in many valleys of the Altyn-tagh, at a height of 11,000 feet, Prejevalsky found the water brackish. The water of the Tarim must therefore contain a larger proportion of salt than any other of the larger rivers of the world; and the unusual amount of evaporation, continued through a great many centuries, must have produced a very large deposit of steppe salts of all kinds. The Chinese from ancient times have called Lob-nor *the* salt lake (κατ' ἐξοχήν), in contradistinction to the many other salt lakes of smaller size. Contrary to theoretical deductions and historical records, we now learn from the first European explorer who has visited the lake, that its water is sweet. Let us endeavour to suggest some explanations.

In winter, when the evaporation is only slight, the river coursing rapidly down to the lake might be expected to diffuse sweet water over the strongly condensed alkali. But, on the other hand, the insignificant depth of the lake would scarcely allow of a dispersion of the salt. A second explanation can be found in the supposition that the reservoir of the waters of the Tarim has undergone changes as to position. Just as rivers in China periodically change their courses, the Tarim may at

different times, have filled parts of the saline, clay steppe with its
overflow, and this becomes all the more probable on reading the
interesting description which Prejevalsky gives of recent occurrences in the river-bed of the Tarim [*vide* p. 99]. Particularly
worthy of attention is the up-raising of the river-bed like that
of the Po and Hoang-ho, above the surrounding plain; allowing
the natives to draw off the water for fishing purposes, [*vide*
p. 102], and assisting the river to change its course by bursting
through its embankments at flood times. In this way the
Tarim may have left its easterly channel, as hitherto marked
on our maps, and the present river flowing to the south-east, with
the two lake basins at its end, perhaps from the neighbourhood
of Akhtarma, may be of comparatively recent origin. In such
case, the earlier lake bed had a more northerly situation than
at present, and became dried up in course of time.

A third and likelier explanation is that besides the two water
basins seen by Prejevalsky, there remains a third communicating
with the Tarim by an arm. A wide experience of Chinese maps,
has taught me that although wanting in practical detail, nothing
is ever laid down that does not actually exist. Now if we consider that the positions of the towns of Karashahr and Korla, as
marked on those maps, are only slightly altered by the new
observations, and that the districts to the south are placed
according to their relative position and distance from both those
places, we may impose some confidence in the accuracy of the
Chinese delineation of this region. From the place where on
Prejevalsky's map the Ugen-daria unites with the Tarim, with
reference to its distance from Korla on the Chinese map, a road
(certainly identical with that taken by Prejevalsky) leads across
the Tarim's eastern course away in a southerly direction.
Whilst Prejevalsky places the river to the south of this road,
the Chinese map takes no notice of such a channel, but continues the Tarim nearly east to a great lake, not marked by
Prejevalsky, which (if shifted to agree with the displacement of
Korla) will be intersected in its one-third northern part by the
41st parallel. This lake is called on the Chinese map Lop-chor
or Lop-noor; and to the north and south of it are situated seven
smaller lakes, the northern of which are called *tsan-hu* (grass or

reed-lakes), whilst those on the south have various names. The map also shows farther to the south-east, and wholly unconnected with the Tarim, another lake called Khas-omo, the centre of which is about 3° east and 1¼° south of Korla, not far from where Prejevalsky places Kara-koshun.[7] The question suggests itself if this Khas-lake does not answer to the black *Koshun* of Prejevalsky.[8]

This would involve the following, *that the Tarim formerly had only one easterly course to the true great Lob-nor, but later at the place where it is now joined by the Ugen-daria, it threw off a branch to the S.E. which became the main river; and that this branch discharged into the once isolated Khas-lake, enlarged it and made it the chief reservoir.*

Many arguments may be adduced in support of this presumption besides those already mentioned.

(*a*) The Chinese map represents plains south of Lob-nor, but mountains south of the Khas-lake, and these with reference to the positions of Prejevalsky's lake and Korla occupy the same place that the Altyn-tagh mountains do.

(*b*) South of Khas-lake the main road to the east leads in the direction of Sha-chau, and from it another branches off southward to Tibet, just as on Prejevalsky's map both roads are placed to the south of Kara-koshun.

[7] The Chinese map to which we have referred gives a second and nameless lake west of Khas-omo. But as none of the earlier maps have it, and as it corresponds in almost every respect to Khas-omo, it is probable that owing to some error the latter lake has been delineated twice over. Though I know of no other instance of the kind, I conjectured this to have been an error even before Prejevalsky's journey, inserting both lakes, however reluctantly, on the map accompanying my work on China.

[8] It must always be a matter of uncertainty if similarity of sound denotes true etymological affinity. "Khas-omo" is Mongolian and means Nephrite or Jade lake, probably to betoken the colour of the water, perhaps too referring to the commerce in Jade which centered in this region. The Turks pronounce it Kash—"Kara-Kash" is a common kind of jade—and "Kara-Koshun" may have been derived from the Mongolian "Khas." On the other hand the Chinese write the name of the district Kara-ho-chau (pronounced Kara-Kodsho). It should be observed, however, that this name is very generally applied to various Mahommedan districts, e. g. to one S.E. of Turfan.

(c) Prejevalsky found that the name of Lob-nor was not applied to either of his lakes, although, from the inquiries of Shaw, Forsyth, and others, it is well known far and wide. But he met with it, evidently without learning its exact meaning, at that part of the Tarim to the east of which the true Lob-nor must lie.

(d) Concurrent historical notices on the former trade-routes from China to the west point with certainty to the conclusion that the region of the true Lob-nor was undisturbed by them, and that they crossed much farther to the south and west of Khas-omo, so that there, and not at Lob, lie the kingdoms of Leulan, Shen-shen, &c., which are named in history as situated near "the salt-lake."

(e) A last and weighty argument is furnished by the only hydrographical measurements taken by Prejevalsky of the rivers observed by him. Taking the fathom at six feet he found :—

	Breadth in feet.	Depth in feet.	Velocity of current.
1. Koncheh-daria . .	42-60	10-14	?
2. Inchikeh-daria . .	?	?	?
3. Ugen-daria . . .	48-60	?	?
4. Tarim, at the mouth of Ugen-daria . .	300-360	20	rapid
5. Tarim, below the confluence of all its feeders . . .	180-210	21	moderate.
6. Tarim, between the two lakes . . .	125	14	170 feet per minute.

It appears, then, that the united river only brings down a part (probably less than half) of the aggregate volume of water contained in all its branches. Even at the time of the greatest summer heat, such a diminution, owing to excessive evaporation, would be difficult to explain; but since the observations were made in winter, when the temperature during the day never rose above freezing-point, and at night fell below zero Fahr., evaporation could have nothing to do with it.

Now Prejevalsky's route lay between two separate arms of the river, it is therefore possible that the eastern arm discharges part of its water by a channel not seen by him, flowing eastwards to an impassable salt desert to which the name Lob-nor heard by him, but so mysteriously passed over, may refer.

If it may be assumed as a certainty that a sweet-water lake, which lies in a steppe of saline loam, and does not serve as a passage for a river like Kara-buran, but allows the water it receives to evaporate, must be of recent origin, our argument with reference to Prejevalsky's Kara-koshun will be confirmed.

We must picture to ourselves the Khas-lake as in former times a small salt-water basin fed by tributaries from the Altyn-tagh and by the Cherchen-daria, and the considerable extension of its area by the irruption of the Tarim, at a comparatively recent period owing to a deflection from its earlier and only eastern course.

The saline morasses on its banks seem to be the remains of its earlier condition. This appears to be the most natural explanation, and it is moreover confirmed by the uncertainty of the later Chinese descriptions. Now they speak of a lake with a circumference of 400 li. Again Lob-nor is said to be a district which it took an army (under Kien-long) two months to march round, and that it consists of steppes and marshy tracts. The whole region too is represented by lakes and salt bogs.

Highly as we must value that which Prejevalsky has accomplished for the exploration of Lob-nor, we cannot yet consider the problem for which he has endured such hardships as finally solved.

7. *Inhabitants of Lob-nor district and political relations.*— Disconnected reports have from time to time come down to us of the existence of one or more states south of Lake Lob. These states attained their highest pitch of prosperity during the Han dynasty ; for then, as we have said, the traffic to the West passed wholly, or at all events in a great measure, through this region. The first to become acquainted with them from China was Chang-kien. In his report to the Emperor, he says, " On the salt lake lie the unwalled places and towns

of Leu-lan and Ku-shi,' 5000 li distant from Chang-ngan
(then the capital of China)." They were at that time under the
dominion of the Huns, and immediately to the south lay the
Tibetan province of Kiang. Soon afterwards, when the Huns
were driven out, this district, together with the whole basin of
the Tarim, fell into the hands of the Chinese, who, with the
exception of a short interval, continued masters of the country
for more than two centuries.

Little mention is made of Kushi, but the ancient annals
and those of the later Han dynasty often refer to the kingdom
of Leu-lan. In the former we find that "Leu-lan is reckoned
to contain about 1500 families. The people go in search of
pasturage to supply their camels, horses, and asses; they
obtain their means of subsistence from the neighbouring countries: their habits are the same as those of the Tibetans, their
neighbours on the south. Precious stones, reeds, pasturage, and
different kinds of trees are found there." [1] In later times the
little kingdom was called by the Chinese Shen-shen, and under
that name it is often mentioned. Yu-ni was the residence of
the prince. It appears that the new name comprised a much
larger district, for it is stated that 14,000 families and 8000
troops were included in it. The lake, though generally marked
as the salt lake, is at times also mentioned as Pului-hai (after a
place of that name), Pu-chang-hai, and so on.

After the downfall of the Han dynasty in the west, we hear
little more of the small state at Lob. Its only visitors were
occasional Buddhist pilgrims on their journeys to Turan and
India, who have left merely short notices of it behind them. In
399 A.D. Fa-hian travelled through it. "Many evil spirits," he
says, "are there, and burning sirocco winds which kill all who
encounter them; neither birds are to be seen in the air, nor
animals on the land. There are no other means of finding the
road than by guiding oneself by the bones of those who have

---

[9] Considering the very small number of names with which we have to
deal here, the recurrence of analogous designations is of course not acci-
dental. We are able to place Kushi at Khas, and Koshun, and hence
infer that the Mongolian tribe of the Khoshotes had their proper seat at
Lob-nor.

[1] Tsien-Han-shn, after De Guignes' *History of the Huns*, i. p. 14.

perished there." Of the little state itself, he reports, " The country of Shen-shen is mountainous and uneven, the soil bare and unfruitful, and the manners of the inhabitants as rude as their clothing, resembling, however, those of the Chinese. The people are Buddhists, about 4000 of them being priests." The similarity of their customs to those of the Chinese, which impressed itself upon the traveller, is doubtless due to the ascendency of the latter, and to their frequent journeys along the great trade routes of those days. That the population had considerably increased is evident from the circumstance of there being four thousand priests; although the ascetic monks may have considered the little country, or the neighbouring mountain range, from its desert character, peculiarly sacred, and suitable for the site of a convent. A short mention is made of the country by the Samaneans, Hwei-sung and Sung-yun, who in the year 518 travelled through it on their journey to the west, and the next to tell us of it is Pei-kiu (607), who was sent by the last princes of the Sui dynasty to Kan-chau-fu, at that time the focus of the Central Asian trade with China, to obtain information concerning the roads along which the merchandise of the different countries was carried, in order to prepare for further conquests. He found that there were three great trade routes, two of which followed the same direction as far as Lob, before dividing into a northern and southern road, whilst the third led viâ Hami. In the year 645 the greatest of all the Buddhist pilgrims, Hwen-thsang, returned from India. Detailed as all his descriptions are of every other part of his journey, he gives only a scanty report of the last places he visited, and contents himself in the Lob-nor region with the bare mention of Nafopo, answering to the ancient Leu-lan. Stan. Julien has shown that this is a name of Indian origin, which probably for some time took the place of the older nomenclature.[2] The annals of the Tang dynasty, as far as they are known, scarcely notice these countries on Lob-nor, and from 750 they are almost forgotten, owing to the decline of the Chinese power in the west.

---

[2] [Col. Yule says that it looks like Sanscrit, and, if so, carries ancient Indian influence to the verge of the great Gobi. *Marco Polo*, 2nd ed. vol. i. 204.—M.]

Once, in the year 940, an emperor sent an embassy to the King of Yu-tien (Khoten), to claim him as a vassal, showing how far the influence of the Chinese had fallen. The difficult and dangerous journey lasted two years, and only after five years' stay did the envoys attempt the return journey. On the way back they followed their former route as far as Tun-hwang; but between this place and Yu-tien places are named which have never been mentioned either before or since, leading us to infer that, in consequence of the dangers caused by hostile tribes, a more southerly road, to which I shall presently return, was pioneered.

The extraordinary rapidity with which the Mohammedan religion spread over Central Asia may have been one of the reasons for the complete ebb of information in the eighth century concerning the roads leading past Lob-nor, for the road *viâ* Hami and along the southern foot of the Tian-shan, now came into more and more exclusive use. And the constant process of desiccation going on in the oases situated along the southern margin of the Tarim basin appears also to have diverted the great trade from them. Even from so early a period as the Mongol supremacy we have no record of any Chinese travellers in these countries. Most of them took a much more northerly route. Thus it happens that the next information we receive is from the west—from no less a personage than Marco Polo, " the Prince of mediæval travellers," who in 1272 explored the above-mentioned route through the desert of Lob. In his narrative, too, the little country of Lob appears as an oasis, which broke the journey through the desert. Shah Rukh's envoys give us a similar idea of it, for they also journeyed homeward through the country on Lake Lob.

And this brings us to modern times. Some of Kang-hi's (1662 —1723) campaigns, and the great conquests of Kien-long (1736 —1796), again directed attention to the west. More geographical works appeared in which the countries on Lake Lob are often described. Only a few of these treatises have been translated into European languages, and amongst them the Hsi-yu-wunn-kien-lu, written in 1723, to which we have referred. In it we find, " Two places, each of 500 houses, are situated on the lake." The inhabitants occupy themselves neither with agriculture nor with rearing cattle, but only in fishing; they make fur coats of swan's-down, weave linen of wild hemp, and bring their fish to the town of Korla for sale. They will neither eat bread nor meat, because it disagrees with them; they speak the Turkish language, but are not Mohammedans."[3] The last statement, which is manifestly incorrect, may have originated in the circumstance that the Mohammedans were unwilling to recognize as their co-religionists the uncivilized inhabitants of the lake region because of their lax observance of their religious rites.

A later work[4] gives remarkable particulars founded on a report dated in the sixth year of the Emperor Kien-long (1741). After mentioning that Lake Lob has a great circumference, and that forty years ago it took an army two months to march round it, it is stated that the country is divided into two districts, viz. Kara-kul and Kara-kodsho. The whole region is under three Begs. The people eat no corn, but live on fish; they weave raiments of wild hemp, and have no similarity of language with other Turks; they attain a great age, often exceeding a hundred years. There are now living 2160 men and women, and 200 of the former are enrolled in banners, i. e. do military service. It takes not quite one month to go from Tun-hwang to the lake. There is one more account of the twenty-third year of Kien-long (1758), in which it is stated that of 2000 people who had formerly lived here, only 600 now were left.

All these notices, scattered through a period of 2000 years, give us in the main a nearly identical representation. A small people, at times numbering several thousand souls, at others again diminishing to a few hundreds, live completely cut off from the rest of the world in the midst of extensive deserts, near a great salt lake, which is the distinguishing feature of the district. Peculiar physical conditions hitherto difficult of explanation, caused their little country, up to the seventh century a converging point for the trade routes, to become more and more isolated as these fell into disuse, and in course of time to be less

[3] According to Hyacinthe's translation in Timkowski's travels, i. 396.
[4] The above-mentioned Hsi-yu-shui-tau-ki.

visited. The inhabitants, in common with the rest of the people
of the Tarim basin, changed their religion, first to Buddhism and
then to Islamism.   Politically they always voluntarily placed
themselves under the ruling power for the time being, seldom
subject to Khoten, sometimes under Chinese dominion, and in
the intermediate periods probably exchanging their dependence
from one to the other of the more northerly situated oasis-states.
Of their mode of life we are only told that they kept horses,
asses, and camels. Much later we hear of their fishing, which
afterwards came to be their chief source of livelihood.   With
regard to the exact locality, we are always referred to the same
district, for it is particularly stated that the various names, such
as Leu-lan, Shen-shen, Nafopo, are included in it, and here and
there the distances from other places are given, so that the position can be approximately determined.   The most detailed in
this respect are the notices on Leu-lan, dating from the Han
dynasty.   They lead us particularly to the conclusion that
the little kingdom lay to the south or south-west of Khas-omo
of the Chinese maps, i. e. Prejevalsky's Kara-koshun, but that
the immediate environs of the great salt lake were uninhabited.

The report of an eye-witness of European culture, and endowed
with a rare spirit of inquiry, concerning so peculiarly situated a
people must claim our special attention.   At one stroke the people of Lob-nor have been placed within reach of our immediate
knowledge, and we find them so little changed from the picture
history has given of them, that Prejevalsky's description often
sounds like an echo of the most ancient Chinese records.
As their geographers of the last century represented, so also
he found the population divided for administrative purposes
into two divisions; the Kara-kultsi (so called after Kara-
kul, a western lake of the Tarim), living on the lower Tarim,
and the Kara-kurchintsi, inhabiting the lakes. The former
number 1200, the latter are now reduced to 300, but a short
time ago amounted to 550 families.   [*Vide supra*, p. 105.]

Prejevalsky's description of the people, their character, manners, customs, and occupations, as well as their sufferings from
the climate, under which they eke out their existence, is one of
the most attractive and interesting ethnological studies with

which recent travellers have furnished us. It, however, only confirms and explains all that we were able to glean from the meagre reports of earlier times. The lesson to be learned in this particular instance is the durability of savage life under the most unfavourable conditions that nature can give.

8. *Observations on Climate.*—The general laws of the climatic conditions of Central Asia are by the deductive method so correctly known, that Prejevalsky's observations only confirm our expectations. [*Vide supra*, p. 124.]

9. *The Land of Cherchen.*—Turning from the observations for which we are indebted to Prejevalsky's journey, to his researches, the chief interest centres in the Cherchen country. Shortly before the Tarim reaches Lake Kara-buran, it receives a right tributary flowing from the south-west, which bears the name of Cherchen-daria, on which is situated a place of the same name. The distance is eleven days' march with pack-asses, estimated by Prejevalsky at 800 versts, which is perhaps a little too high.[5] From Cherchen it is ten days' march to Nai, and three thence to Kiria. Shaw ascertained it to be sixteen instead of thirteen days' march,[6] and his informant was a man who had lived twelve years in Cherchen. He also reported that Cherchen (written Charchand by him), lay on a river which flowed to Lob; he adds that the banks of this river are inhabited, and the road follows the course of the river. The productions of Cherchen, which, according to the foregoing report, are maize and wheat, apple and pear trees, prove the excellence of its climate, even though, as Shaw remarks, its elevation exceed that of Kiria, because rice and cotton do not grow there.

Ciarcian was first known through Marco Polo, who reached it on his road from Khoten to Lob, five days before reaching the latter. The name was again brought to light by Johnson's discovery, in 1866, of a route through Cherchen

---

[5] The day's march of a pack-ass is reckoned in China at forty li. This would make 440 li, or about 220 versts. As Shaw reckons the distance from Cherchen to Lob at six days' march, by taking the above measurement of seventy li as the length of a day's journey, we arrive in this way at nearly a similar result.

[6] Proceedings of the Royal Geographical Society, vol. xvi. p. 247.

to Lob. But we are indebted to Yule for identifying the place and name with Marco Polo's description.[7] Johnson learned that it contained 500 houses, but he obtained, as it appears, no reliable information regarding its distance from Kiria, which he reckoned to be only nine marches. Two marches from the last-named place he gives Nia, a village of fifty houses, which is clearly the Nai of Prejevalsky, although the latter traveller heard of 900 houses.[8]

10. *The Southern and South-western Mountainous Country.*— Nothing is more difficult than to obtain reliable information from natives concerning mountain ranges and their direction, especially when the narrators have only travelled along roads from which the mountains are visible in the distance. Prejevalsky had moreover the disadvantages of meeting with certain distrust, and of not possessing a sufficiently capable interpreter. He gathered that the south-westerly continuation of the Altyn-tagh extended without a break, and, as he therefore appears to assume, as an uninterrupted escarpment of mountainous land, facing towards the lower desert, as far as the oases of Kiria and Khoten. If the only probable explanation of this state-ment lies in the circumstance that mountains can be seen from the road at a greater or less distance, the existence of so

---

[7] Yule's *Marco Polo*, second edition, i. p. 201.

[8] It is curious how rarely itineraries agree with one another as to distances. If it were not for the identification of the names in the authorities here cited (Marco Polo, Johnson, Shaw, and Prejevalsky), a comparison would be scarcely possible. It need not, therefore, surprise us that the accounts of Hwen-thsang, who, coming direct from India, preferred the Sanscrit names introduced with Buddhism to those of the natives, are not in full accordance with others. The terminal points, Yu-tien (Khoten), and Nafopo (Leu-lan), are fixed. Between these he reckons (starting from Yu-tien) 330 li to Peino, which can be identified with Marco Polo's Pein (according to another reading Peym); 200 li to Nijang, the distance of which from Khoten answers to that of Kiria; 400 to the buried cities of the kingdom of Tuholo; 600 li to Nimo or Chemotona, and lastly 1000 li to Nafopo. A comparison of the distance of 530 li from Yu-tien to Nijang with that of 2000 li between the latter place and Nafopo, nearly corresponds with that between Khoten and Kiria on the one side, and from Kiria to Lake Karaburan on the other, so that Nijang and Kiria may without hesitation be considered as nearly identical. Nimo alone remains doubtful; from its position it cannot pass for Cherchen, and it may have altogether disappeared.

unnatural a configuration assumed to be the margin of the
Tarim basin, in the shape of a wall-like range running from
north-east to south-west, becomes improbable, as it also does on
comparing the delineation of the mountains on the Chinese
maps and the information collected by Shaw. Prejevalsky sup-
plements his statement with some particulars which he heard
regarding the mountainous region to the south of the lakes.
[*Vide supra*, p. 83], and apparently assigns the name " Tuguz-
daban " to the supposed great marginal range, and in this sense
it is inserted on Petermann's map accompanying Prejevalsky's
narrative. We have only to observe here that this name
(properly *Tokus-dawan*) signifies " the nine passes," and is not
mentioned now for the first time. Shaw had already heard of
it. He writes it *Tokos-dewan*, is aware of its meaning, and
states that this region of the nine passes is reported to be
situated a fortnight's journey east of Cherchen, and that a road
led through it to Lan-chau-fu, by which Kalmuks came to trade
at Cherchen. Since the places from which the information
relating to Tokus-dawan originates are far apart, and since in
both cases this one name is given to a pass, we must infer that
it is known far and wide; on the other hand, the difference in
the position assigned to it—first, by Prejevalsky, nearly south-
west from the Tarim lakes in the direction of Cherchen; secondly,
by Shaw, fourteen days' journey east of the last-named place—
would seem as if it referred to an extended trade-route, " the road
of nine passes," and not merely to a particular locality. This
is probably a road leading in one direction to Tsaidam, Koko-
nor and Si-ning-fu, in the other to Khoten.

If the evidence adduced in support of the supposed marginal
range must, after what we have said, be rejected, and a different
explanation given of it, besides the extreme improbability of such
a feature in the orography as a wall of mountains running from
south-west to north-east, other positive grounds may be urged
against it. First, we know from the concurrent statements of
Johnson and Shaw, that the road from Kiria departs from its
earlier direction (nearly east by south), makes a sweep round, and
then proceeds nearly due north; the most probable cause for this
deflection is that a more northerly chain of mountains rising in

the west, has to be circumvented. Again, Shaw learned that to the right of the road from Kiria to Cherchen, black, i. e. snowless mountains might be seen at a distance in clear weather; further, that although these mountains were not far from Cherchen and Lob, it took six days' travelling in an east and south direction to get from the former of these places into a range resorted to by hunters, gold-seekers, and shepherds. This may perhaps be explained by the circumstance that arid outlying hills project to the neighbourhood of Cherchen, but that a range suitable for the habitation of men and cattle, would be first met with a greater distance off. We can therefore agree with Shaw that Cherchen lies in a great bay of plain running into the hills.

Summarizing all the results of Prejevalsky's expedition, we find our knowledge of Central Asia by his help wonderfully extended, and our interest in it greatly excited. The problem of the situation of Lob-nor has been very nearly solved, that of the lake basins, into which the greater part, at any rate, of the waters of the Tarim *at present* discharge, is almost explained; the site of the ancient kingdoms of Leu-lan and Shen-shen has been again found, sufficiently explored and described; contrary to views hitherto prevailing, south of the present Tarim lakes, a lofty range, rising to an altitude of 14,000 feet, and perhaps higher towards the south-west, with a steep escarpment on the north, has been discovered, and its function as the northern margin of the Tibetan plateau at this point very probably determined. Moreover our geographical ideas of this region have been materially transposed, and we receive a natural key to explain historical occurrences, whose relation to the configuration of the soil was hitherto obscure. The inhabitants, too, isolated from the rest of the world, have been brought nearer to us than they could ever have been through Chinese sources of information. At the same time we receive from the talented explorer comprehensive and suggestive conclusions on the animal and plant life in its relation to the general character of the region. But the chief merit of Prejevalsky's observations is their comprehensive and many-sided grasp of the subject.

Every new solution, however, brings with it new problems.

The results achieved have brought forward a number of questions which a few years ago could not be formulated. The problem of Lake Lob itself requires more thorough investigation. The discovery of a sweet-water lake near the place where all history speaks of a great salt lake, and where every theoretical inference certainly points to such a conclusion, cannot satisfy us. We are not yet disposed to admit that a precipitous cliff faces the Tarim basin, in this particular spot, without feeling most desirous to know its further continuation, particularly in the direction of the Khoten road which once led through a number of oases, but subsequently fell into disuse, and whose former existence in part revealed by ancient names, has quite recently been re-established; and it would be premature as yet to deduce from these explorations the discovery of a continuous range extending towards Tsaidam and Tibet. To the former of these problems, so far as the southern margin of the Tarim basin is concerned, Count Béla Szeczenyi has dedicated the great journey towards the accomplishment of which, with a noble love of geographical exploration, he has resolved to devote his powers and means for a series of years. The departure of his expedition from Shanghai is imminent. Prejevalsky too, with untiring energy, is about to undertake another journey to elucidate new facts connected with these regions, and if possible to carry out his long-cherished plan of penetrating into Tibet. His travels hitherto may well compare with many of the most remarkable expeditions of modern times on African soil in the fruitfulness of their results, and we may expect from the efforts of both travellers the most important explanations on those parts of Asia which, after the great works of the last two centuries, is most closed to our knowledge.

COLONEL PREJEVALSKY'S REPLIES TO BARON RICHTHOFEN'S CRITICISMS.

BARON RICHTHOFEN, so well known for his travels in China, in a paper read before the Berlin Geographical Society [1] last spring, made some highly interesting remarks on and additions to my short report of a journey to Lob-nor.

. Upon the authority of various Chinese sources of information, Baron Richthofen gave some important particulars of the earlier history of this region, its inhabitants, and the ancient remains discovered by me. But at the same time the learned professor expressed doubts as to whether the lakes which I discovered at the mouth of the Tarim form the true Lob-nor, and whether their position should not be farther north, i. e. due east of the bend of the Tarim, near its confluence with the Ugen-daria.

In the interests of truth, I take the liberty of replying to these criticisms.

The chief arguments adduced by Baron Richthofen, in support of his opinion are the following :—1. That whereas the lakes (Kara-buran and Chon-kul) discovered by me at the mouth of the Tarim contain sweet water, all the accounts dating from the very earliest times represent Lob-nor as a salt lake, and that this is in full accord with scientific deduction. 2. On all Chinese maps the position of Lob-nor is considerably to the north of that which I assigned to it ; and the

---

[1] Bemerkungen zu den Ergebnissen von Oberst-Lieutenant Preje-valski's Reise nach dem Lop-noor und Altyn-tagh.

Lower Tarim flows due east instead of in a south-easterly direction ; and, 3. These same Chinese maps show the country to the south of Lob-nor to be flat, whilst near my lakes they place a small isolated lake—Khas-omo, to the south of which lofty mountains shoot up from the plain in the identical spot where I met with the Altyn-tagh. In order to reconcile the discrepancies between the Chinese statements and the results of my investigations, Baron Richthofen supposes that the Lower Tarim in comparatively recent times altered its course ; a small channel, probably, as the Baron thinks, unexplored by me, continues to follow the former direction to the east towards the true Lob-nor, whilst the chief mass of water diverted to the south-east entered Lake Khas-omo, and here formed with its overflow the lakes which I discovered.

It is impossible to deny that such a phenomenon may have occurred. A river with such a rapid stream as the Tarim flowing in a loose alluvial soil might easily have changed its course. My opinion, however, is that no such important change has occurred within comparatively recent times, but that the contradictory statements of Chinese maps and descriptions of the Lower Tarim and Lob-nor may be readily accounted for *by the misleading and inaccurate information which the Chinese themselves possessed of these localities.*

Let us proceed in due order.

Before we had made many marches to the south of Korla we began to perceive the inaccuracy of existing maps. Thus the Koncheh-daria, instead of making a large and sudden elbow to the west, only slightly inclines in this direction, and then turning to the east and south-east, flows for some distance in an independent channel before joining the Kiok-ala-daria, an arm of the Tarim. The width of the Koncheh-daria where we crossed it a second time (48 versts S.S.W. of Korla) is 50 to 70 ft., depth 10 to 14 ft., and stream moderately rapid Less than ten versts from the Koncheh, we came to another river—the Inchikeh-daria (50 to 70 ft. wide and of some depth) and twenty versts beyond this again, to the Tarim itself at its confluence with the Ugen-daria, a river which takes its rise in the Muzart.

M

Nothing of the kind is to be found on any map hitherto existing compiled (in the absence of European sources of information) from Chinese records. If such inaccuracy as this can be detected at a distance of less than 100 versts from so old a town as Korla and the still more ancient caravan road leading from it along the southern foot of the Tian-Shan—what reliance can be placed in the same Chinese sources regarding more remote and less accessible districts such as the Lower Tarim and Lob-nor ?

That the rivers Koncheh and Inchikeh-daria flow from distinct and widely separated localities can be proved not only by the frequent inquiries we made of the inhabitants—but by the difference in the temperature of their water. In clear weather on the 6/18th November at midday the temperature of the Koncheh water was 33° Fahr., the river was full of small ice, and a few days later, as we learned from the natives, was frozen over ; on the other hand, the Inchikeh water only two days later, i. e. on the 8/20th November, was 37° Fahr., and was not obstructed by ice even at night. The cause of this is evident—the Koncheh-daria flows from the high cold lake of Bagarash, not far from where we crossed, whilst the Inchikeh-daria comes from a distance through a low and warm desert where its water gets heated. Moreover, it is positively certain that the Inchikeh is not an arm of the Tarim, as might have been supposed. Thus in the month of November, when we crossed the former its water was on a level with the banks, its width was about 50 ft., and depth 10 ft. At this time the Tarim was also high. When we returned in the following spring, and crossed the Inchikeh on the 18/30th April, it was 3 to 4 ft. lower than in the preceding autumn, whilst the level of the Tarim was the same as in November. This of course could not have occurred if there had been any communication between the two rivers.

We could not ascertain how the Inchikeh united with the Koncheh. Some of the natives told us that before joining the Koncheh, it passed through a lake ; others said that it disappeared in saline marshes and at flood time flowed straight into the Koncheh. In any case its mouth is not far from the place of our crossing, for our travelling-companion, Zaman Beg, rode to Korla by another road running due north for some distance from the village of Akhtarma and assured us that by this route he had only to cross one river—the Koncheh-daria.

The Tarim, at its confluence with the Ugen-daria, flows in one channel of 350—400 ft. wide, and 20 ft. deep, as we learned from the natives, for we were rarely able to take soundings, and never in the presence of our guides.

It is unnecessary to repeat the statements contained in my report regarding the hydrography of the Lower Tarim, and I will only add that the chief cause of the diminution of the volume of its stream as it flows farther to the south-east, is the diversion of its water into artificial lakes and marshes occupying vast tracts along its lower course, and these, owing to strong evaporation continuing the greater part of the year, absorb an immense quantity of moisture subtracted from the principal river.

Regarding the possibility of there being another channel by which, as Baron Richthofen supposes, the Tarim carries part of its water to the east, and there forms the true Lob-nor—such a supposition is not supported by the facts hitherto obtained. To say nothing of the circumstance that the inhabitants would surely have known of such a channel and so large a lake, and would sooner or later have told me about them, we ourselves followed the bank of the Tarim, and could not detect any, not even the smallest rivulet crossing our road. Had there been one, it would not have escaped our notice, for in crossing such places the camels were always troublesome— nor can the rivers Koncheh and Kiok-ala-daria,[2] along whose left (eastern) bank we did not travel, detach a considerable channel to one side, for if this were the case, the Kiok-ala-daria would not be much larger in its lower course than at the point of its separation from the Tarim.

[2] The Kiok-ala-daria, near the village of the same name, is about 150 ft. wide, and a little lower in its narrowest part, where we crossed it, only 80 ft., whereas 16 versts to the east of the village of Shui-su, and therefore after its confluence with the Koncheh, it is nearly twice its former size (210—230 ft.).

Now with reference to the lakes at the mouth of the chief river, of which there are two : Kara-buran and Kara-kurchin or Chon-kul ;[3] both are shallow and contain fresh water. As regards the former the presence of sweet water can be explained by the fact that the Tarim only flows through it, and its water is therefore constantly renewed.

As to the other enclosed lake basin, it appears at first sight inexplicable why its water should be sweet.[4] But the facts collected by me on the spot explain the apparent anomaly.[5] The fact is, the Chon-kul is nothing more than a wide expanse of land flooded by the Tarim ; in all its western parts I observed a current, sometimes very considerable, towards the north-east. In this part the Tarim preserves an independent channel, although reduced to the size of a large ditch. Here the last two villages[6] of Lob-nortsi are situated, and farther to the north-east lie boundless and impassable tracts of marsh land which actually absorb the remainder of the Tarim water. In these marshes, and in the great salt bogs extending, as the natives told us, far away in a N.E. direction, the standing water is doubtless salt, just as it is along the shallow western margin of the Chon-kul.

In ancient times, when this lake was much larger, it may possibly have united with Kara-buran, and submerged all the salt bogs along its southern shore. At that time, probably, the belt of stagnant, and therefore salt water must have been wider than at present,[7] and this may have induced the Chinese writers to call it " the salt lake."

Regarding the circumstance of the natives not knowing or

---

[3] Erroneously printed Chok-kul in my report and accompanying map which I was unable personally to revise.

[4] I regret extremely that in my short report hastily written at Kulja, I should have omitted to state the causes of the sweetness of the Lob-nor water.

[5] The water of the Tarim is in no part in the slightest degree salt, and the same remark applies to the rivers Koncheh, Inchikeh, Ugen and Cherchen darias.

[6] Both are called Kara-Kurchin.

[7] At present the water of Chon-Kul is salt for a distance of 300 paces from the shores, more or less.

rather not employing the term "Lob-nor" for these lakes, a parallel may be shown in the case of the Tarim.   The inhabitants hardly ever call it by this name, but generally speak of it as the Yarkand-daria or Chon-daria,[*] the name Lob-nor is applied by these very people to the whole inhabited district of Kara-kul and Kara-kurchin.   When we arrived at the first Tarim village of Kutmet-kul, the chief of the place, in answer to my question, "How far is it to Lob-nor?" answered, pointing to himself, "I am Lob-nor."

In conclusion, I consider it my duty to repeat that the inhabitants one and all denied the existence of any other lakes in the neighbouring desert besides those on which they lived. They likewise did not know of the oasis of "Gast," about which I had so often heard in Tsaidam.

N. PREJEVALSKY.

18/30th August, 1878.
Village of Otradnoi, Government of Smolensk.

[*] This means, " Great river."

APPENDIX.

FAUNA OF THE TARIM VALLEY AND LOB-NOR.

Mammalia.

TIGER, common, in some places numerous.

Manul (*felis manul*), common.

Lynx, reported to be occasionally seen.

Wolf, } unfrequent, even rare.
Fox, }

Common otter, said to be tolerably numerous by the banks of the fish-lakes.

Hedgehog, rare.

Shrew, rare.

Deer (*Cervus maral*), common.

Steppe antelope (*A. subgutturosa*), common.

Hare, tolerably numerous.

Meriones, two species, one rare, the other numerous in places.

Wild boar, common, in some places numerous.

Mice, few.

Wild camel (*Camelus bactrianus, ferus*), inhabits the region to the east of Lob-nor, and occasionally the sand-wastes on the Lower Tarim.

Avi-Fauna.

The following is a list of birds observed in the Tarim valley during winter:—

Grey vulture, a visitant from the Tian Shan.

Eagles, two kinds (*fulva* and *bifasciata*), very rare.

Buzzard, only once seen.

Goshawk, rare.

Sparrowhawk, common.

Merlin, rare.

Kestrel, common, habitant.

Marsh harrier,
Common harrier, } habitants ; probably also wintering.

Long-eared owl,
Short-eared owl, } rare.

Athene plumipes, only found at Chargalyk.

Raven (*O. corax*), habitant, rare.

Hooded or Royston crow (*O. cornix*), only a few specimens observed at Chargalyk ; this being the extreme eastern limit of its range.

Eastern crow (*O. orientalis*), habitant, numerous.

Magpie (*Pica caudata var.*), habitant, rare.

Biddulph's Podoces (*Podoces Biddulphii*), habitant, common.

Sparrows, { *Passer montanus*,
           { *P. ammodendri*, } habitants.

Bullfinch (*Carpodacus rubicilla*), winters in small numbers.

Rosefinch (*Erythrospiza obsoleta*), habitant, rare.

  „ { *Cynchramus schœniclus*,
     { *C. pyrrhuloides*, } habitants, common.

Black-throated thrush (*T. atrigularis*), winters, numerous.

Myophoneus Temminckii, winters, very rare.

Redstart (*Ruticilla erythronota*), winters, very rare.

Rhopophilus deserti, n. sp., common, habitant.

Azure Titmouse, *Cyanistes cyanus*, habitant, rare.

Bearded Titmouse, *Panurus barbatus*, very numerous, habitant.

Leptopœcile Sophiœ, rare.

Meadow-pipit (*Anthus pratensis ?*), rarely winters, nidifies.

Skylark (*Alauda arvensis*), very rare, habitant.

Pale short-toed Larks (*Alaudula leucophœa*), habitant, numerous.

Crested Lark (*Galerita magna*), habitant, numerous.

Homeyer's shrike (*Lanius Homeyeri ?*), winters, rare.

Hoopoe (*Upupa epops*), winters, only met with at Chargalyk.

Woodpeckers (*Picus sp.*), habitant, very common.

Sand-grouse (*Syrrhaptes paradoxus*), rare, habitant.

Turtle-dove (*Turtur vitticollis*[1], T. sp.), only met with at Chargalyk.

Harelda glacialis, *Anas clypeata*, Cormorant (*Carbo cormoranus*), Brown-headed Gull (*Larus brunneicephalus*),	rare, only single specimens seen in November.
Common bittern (*Botaurus stellaris*), Swan (*Cygnus olor ?*)	said to winter in small numbers among the reedy unfrozen parts of Lob-nor.

[1] [Called in Kashmir *Kookail*.—M.]

[N.B.—Many of the birds here mentioned will be found described and some figured in "Lahore to Yarkand," by Henderson and Hume, and in Blanford's "Ornithological Notes to Eastern Persia."—M.]

LAKE BALKASH.

Earliest notices—Origin of name—First surveys—Russian explorers—Assanoff; Schrenk—Incorrect cartography—Fordoroff's observations—Height of lake and relative position —Rivers flowing into it; the Ili and its headwaters the Tekes—Muzart pass—Kulja and its neighbourhood—The Lepsa—Chubar-agatch valley—The Kara-tal—Buddhistic remains—Nifantieff deputed to survey Lake Balkash—Preparations; he launches his boats—Difficulties—He constructs a felt dam; arrives at the lake; begins survey —His assistant shipwrecked—He completes survey following year.

It was not till the final occupation of the district of Semirechinsk (or seven rivers [1]) in 1849, that the Russians seriously thought about surveying and exploring Lake Balkash. Up to that time all that had been done was to survey parts of the shores and collect the scattered notices of the few who had visited it. The earliest information given of the lake is contained in the Chinese records, the relations of this people with Central Asia from very remote times having acquainted them first with its geography.

Si-yui or the western country in the widest

[1] The seven rivers are the Ayaguz, Lepsa, Ak-su, Bien, Kara tal, Kok-su, and Ili.

sense comprised the whole extent of the continent
of Asia to the west of the Great Wall, and was
known to the Chinese in the second century, B.C.—
In the year of our Lord, 607, Pei-kiu, inspector of
foreigners, compiled special maps of forty-four
states at that time existing in Central Asia; but
none of these maps and descriptions are extant,
and from the confusion in the terminology, owing
partly to the changes in the names of towns and
countries at different epochs and partly no doubt
to the inaccessibility of Chinese sources of information, and the comparatively little attention
hitherto bestowed on them, opinions widely diver-
gent prevailed, even down to recent times.

Humboldt says in his "Asie Centrale," (vol.
ii. p. 64), that the Chinese called Lake Balkash
Si-hai or Western Sea, which led to its being
confounded with the Caspian, and a Bavarian
geographer, Spruner, in 1855, actually gave it that
name on his map. The name Balkash-nor, by
which it is at present known, originated with the
the Dzungars, a people who are rapidly becoming
extinct under the influence of the terrible wars
which have desolated the border states of China
and Russia. This is the name also given to it
by Klaproth on his great map of Central Asia
compiled in 1833, from the surveys of the
Jesuit missionaries (*supra*, p. 137). Amongst
the Kirghiz it was generally known as "Den-
ghiz" or "Tenghiz," a word meaning "sea."
In the great survey of Russia, published in the

sixteenth century, Balkash is not mentioned, although some of the great inland water basins, as for instance the Aral, are tolerably accurately described. But on the general map of Siberia, supposed to have been compiled about the year 1695, Lake Balkash appears as the "Tenghiz Sea," with the rivers Syr and Amun-daria flowing from its west shore into the Aral. If we consider the difficulties of obtaining correct information in those days, it is wonderful how accurate this map of Siberia appears to be.

The occupation of the line of the Irtysh, strengthened by a chain of forts and outposts extending from Omsk to Ust Kamennogorsk (1716-19), opened a wide field to geographical enterprise. Disputes frequently arose as to the ownership of the annexed lands of the Dzungarians, to settle which the Russian Government caused careful topographical surveys and maps to be made. In this way the country became better known. Special missions, too, were from time to time sent to the independent princes. Thus we read of the boyard Marémianoff being charged to carry an autograph letter from the Tsar Peter the Great to Tsevan Araptan, lord of Dzungaria, on which occasion Prince Gagarin, Governor of Siberia, furnished another member of the mission with special instructions to observe everything that he saw on the road to the *urga* or camp of the prince, and keep a journal.

In 1748 Lieutenant Podzoroff, was sent from

fort Yamish with two official letters to the khan; his diary is full of information regarding the country visited and the actual state of affairs in Dzungaria; the following year, another officer, Lieutenant Tiersky, was despatched on a similar mission by the commandant of fort Yamish.[2] Trained surveyors, too, accompanied the caravans of merchandise, and they were instructed to make route surveys of the country traversed and collect information upon the neighbouring districts. From these and other materials good maps were compiled in the eighteenth century of the river basin of the Irtysh and the country occupied by the Kalmuks of Dzungaria.

But notwithstanding the activity displayed in this direction, no Russian traveller appears to have visited Lake Balkash, and the information concerning it in the early part of the present century was probably derived from hearsay and conjecture.[3] Between the years 1837-43, however, the whole extent of the trans-Irtysh steppe as far as the rivers Ayaguz and Chu was mapped on a scale of five versts to the inch, and at the same time the north-western and southern shores of Lake Balkash were explored and surveyed from Cape Chaukkar to the estuary of the Ili.

[2] The narratives of Lieuts. Podzoroff and Tiersky are published in the *Vestnik* of the Imperial Geographical Society for 1851, part iii. No. 6, p. 60.

[3] As we learn from an article by General Babkoff in the *Zapisky*, from which we borrow these particulars.

In 1839 Prince Gortchakoff, at that time governor of Western Siberia, sent an officer of Cossacks by the name of Assanoff with a small force of men to Lake Balkash, to inquire into the possibility of establishing a fishing-station.   In September, 1839, Assanoff left Ayaguz, and, descending the river of that name, reached the lake whose northern and eastern shores he explored from the estuary of the Ayaguz to that of the Lepsa—taking soundings and trying the fishing. He only found two kinds of fish, the marena [4] and sudak,[5] and these not in any large numbers, the brackish water rendering it uninhabitable for the cartilaginous fishes.   Owing to this and other considerations the fishery scheme was abandoned.

Between 1840-43 Schrenk, whose valuable observations have contributed so much to science, but of whose travels, alas, no detailed narrative has been published,[6] explored the south-eastern, north-western, and southern shores of Lake Balkash.   The want of a complete and systematic survey, however, continued to be felt, and became manifest in the inaccuracy of existing maps.

[4] The genus *marena*, according to Webster, takes its name from Lake Morin, in the marsh of Brandenburg, in Prussia.

[5] The common pike-perch, *Lusioperca sandra*, well known on the Neva, where it is highly esteemed for its delicate white flesh.

[6] Except the extracts published in *Beiträge zur Kenntniss des Russischen Reichs*.   Baer und Helmersen.

Thus on Pansner's map, published in 1816, Lake
Balkash is represented as an ellipse, with the
longer axis lying in a meridional direction, and, as
Pansner was the standard authority of those days,
other cartographers copied his mistakes.   On
Arrowsmith's map, published in 1822, the longitude
of the lake is incorrectly given as 71° (on Pansner's
map 76°), and serious blunders occur in the
names, for instance the Ili is called " *Uliya*," an
ancient stone building is represented as a town,
and so on.   Klaproth's large map of Central Asia
reduces Lake Balkash by one third of its actual
size, and erroneously shows a considerable extent
of marshy country to the north.   But the general
fault of all cartographers lay in the delineation of
its length, which, according to the latest surveys,
has been ascertained to be about 330 miles, with
an area ascertained by Veniukoff to be 19,600 sq.
versts = 8612 English sq. miles.'

. No astronomical observations to fix its position
cartographically had been taken down to 1834.
About that time, however, observations were commenced in the more inhabited parts of Siberia,
and it was to connect these that the Government

' The width varies from 5 miles in its northern part to 50
towards the south ; the circumference is about 880 miles.   The
depth nowhere exceeds 56 ft., and shallows and sand-banks of a
mile or more in extent are of frequent occurrence.   On the
north, north-east, and north-west the shores are hilly, whilst on
the south a wide, uneven plain extends to the foot of the Ala-tau
mountains.

decided on obtaining a sufficient number of astronomically-fixed positions. Accordingly we find Feodoroff deputed for this task in 1832. By 1837 he had fixed no less than seventy-nine positions, and amongst them one on Lake Balkash at the mouth of the Lepsa. On the 29th September, 1834, he arrived at the town of Ayaguz, which three years previously had become the centre of an administrative district; deep snow covering the Tarbagatai mountains, and dearth of fodder for his horses, owing to the lateness of the season, prevented him from exploring the sources of the Ayaguz river, and its estuary becoming lost in reedy swamps, about ten miles from the lake, was quite inaccessible for scientific purposes. Feodoroff, therefore, after fixing the position of the town of Ayaguz (now the Central Ayaguz outpost), resolved on descending the Lepsa. Having completed his arrangements, he set out for Lake Balkash on the 7th October, 1834. Ten miles from Ayaguz he crossed to the left bank of the river of the same name, and continued to descend its valley, passing the tomb of Kuzu-Kerpetch,[a] famous for its Kirghiz legend, which still lives in the recollection of the inhabitants. Turning the Arganatau mountains on the west, Feodoroff gained the Lepsa on the 12th October, and on the 17th of that

---

[a] Kuzu-Kerpetch was the name of a Kirghiz chief celebrated in the folk-songs for his valour and for his love for Baian Sulu, who became the cause of his death.

month reached its estuary in Lake Balkash. Here he took eight lunar zeniths, and two occultations of stars, finding the mouth of the Lepsa to be in 46° 20′ 3″ N. lat., and 48° 0′ 5″ longitude east of Pulkovo observatory. Important as Feodoroff's work was for correcting the position of Lake Balkash, no further observations of the sort have since been made, and the subsequent topographical surveys which, as we shall see, were undertaken at the cost of great labour and expense, lose much of their value, owing to the want of fixed cartographical positions.

The height of the lake above sea-level has never yet been accurately determined. Humboldt thought it could not be more than 1800 feet. Semeonoff, however, according to calculations based on his experiments made with boiling water on the river Ili, and on Lake Ala-kul, estimates it at between 600 and 700 feet.

There can be no doubt that the whole country west of the Altai gradually slopes to the Caspian Sea, and forms almost one continuous depression, distinctly defined by Lake Balkash, the hungry steppe, and the row of lakes on the lower Chu and Sari-su. Semeonoff is of opinion that Lakes Balkash and Ala-kul were, at one time, part of the same basin, of which the latter is the desiccated end, and his view is corroborated by the presence of the brackish channel of Aitaktin-Karakum, directed from the west shore of Ala-kul towards Balkash.

From the brief summary we have given of the explorations on Lake Balkash, it will be seen that they were of a partial character and that no general survey of the lake had yet been made. This want was supplied in 1851-52 under the auspices of General Hasford, Governor of Western Siberia. But before acquainting our readers with some details of this expedition, let us take a glance at the rivers which empty themselves into the lake.

Of these the most important is the Ili, which, under the name of Tekes, rises on the northern slope of the Tian Shan, at a height of 11,600 feet above sea-level, and flows first in a N.N.E. direction, through wild mountain gorges. On issuing into the plain at the foot of the Tian Shan, it turns to the east, and receives a number of tributaries, whose transverse valleys lead up to the celebrated Muzart or Mussart pass,[*] by which

[*] The Muzart Pass was explored in 1867 by Poltoratsky, in 1870 by Baron Kaulbars, and in the following year by Captain Shepeleff, who descended the glacier on its southern slope as far as the Kashgarian frontier. It may be remarked here that the word Muzart, or Mussart, means "snowy," and is not properly applicable to any one pass in particular; but is a term used by the natives to denote any of the snowy passes of the Tian Shan. This pass was formerly the only means of communication between the Chinese province of Ili (Dzungaria) and Kashgar, and it was kept in excellent order. Since the Mohammedan insurrection, however, and the capture of Kulja, the road was little used, fell into bad order, and became almost impassable. According to Schuyler, the Russians occupied it in 1871 (*Turkistan*, ii. 319). This was the route followed by the old Buddhist pilgrim, Hwen Thsang.

N

the road from Kulja to Aksu, crosses the Tian Shan. From the mouth of its left tributary, the Kara-ussu, the Tekes turns to the N.E., and bursts through the northern spurs of the Tian Shan, and on being joined by the Kunges it proceeds northwards, taking the name of Ili. Further on it receives another important tributary on the right, and immediately afterwards turns westward, nearly at right angles with its former course, and flows past the city of Ili, Kulja, or Guldja, situated on its high right bank, 1930 li from Urumtsi, and 10,820 li (about 3700 miles) distant from Peking. Kulja was, under Chinese rule, an important emporium of trade and the administrative centre for the unruly tribes of the Eleuths, Turgutes, &c. It was visited and described by the Russian traveller Putimtseff, in 1811, before the rebellion broke out which put an end to the power of the Chinese. Since it passed into Russian hands (1871), it has been visited by several Europeans, notably by Mr. Schuyler, who has given a most interesting account of his stay there. Kulja was a place of great importance from a very early period, when it was known as " Ili-balik," i. e. city of Ili.[1] The

---

[1] Ili is "resplendent," so Ili-balik is resplendent city. Ritter also calls it Almalik, but Semeonoff in a note to the Russian edition of Ritter's *Asien*, says that Amalik (or " apple city," from the apple orchards around it,) lay forty versts W.N.W. of Kulja, probably near the ruins of the modern Alimtu, on the banks of a stream of the same name.

Emperor Kien-Long, who rebuilt it in 1754, gave it
the honorary title of Hoi-Yuan-cheng. Amongst
the Kirghiz it was commonly called "Guldja,"
a word of Mongol or Manchu origin, signifying
mountain-goat (*Capra ammon*), an animal formerly
met with in the neighbourhood. Two hours'
ride from the town are the mountains of Khongor,
abounding in iron and coal. The river, having
changed its direction, now flows close under the
walls of the town with a very swift stream, and
the only means of crossing it is in boats. Hence
it pursues its course through a wide, well-culti-
vated, and fertile valley till it enters the plain that
extends between the southern spurs of the Semirechinsk mountains on the north, and the trans-
Ili Alatau on the south, and joins Lake Balkash
upwards of 400 miles below Kulja, by three arms
forming a large delta. The river is navigable for
about fifty miles above Kulja, and was used by
the Chinese as a means of supplying their garrison
with provisions, but the attempts to navigate it
from Lake Balkash have hitherto proved unsuccessful.[*] Its total length from the sources of the Tekes
in the Muzart to Lake Balkash is about 750 miles.

The river next in importance flowing into Lake
Balkash is the Lepsa, or Lep-si of the Chinese,
whose three sources rise amid the eternal snows on
the north-west slope of the Semirechinsk Alatau,

[*] For an account of the attempts made to navigate the Ili,
see Schuyler's *Turkistan*, ii. 152.

near the Kukeh-tau-daban,[3] whence they flow
into wild gorges between walls of granitic and
crystalline rocks, before uniting in the cleft or
valley of Chubar-agatch,[4] in which stands the
Lepsinsky Stanitza, or settlement of Lepsa,
founded in 1855. The valley, which is 2700 feet
above sea-level, is oval and surrounded on all
sides by lofty mountains. Its climate and soil
are favourable to colonization, although the
former has its drawbacks, for the currents of
winds from the mountains blow with great
violence, and fogs and mists often prevent the
sun's rays from penetrating and warming the
atmosphere; pasturage, however, is abundant and
excellent, and trees in great variety—fir, ash,
white birch, apple, rock cherry, mountain ash,
guelder rose, barberry, black and scarlet haw-
thorne, &c., grow luxuriantly. Here in 1859
there were 448 houses, tenanted by 2394 persons
of both sexes, who occupied themselves chiefly
with agriculture, and who could boast good crops
of millet, wheat, and flax.[5]

[3] *I. e.* 'pass of the blue peak.'　General Abramoff says that
the Lepsa has but two sources, known by the name of Terekti,
uniting below the Chubar-agatch Valley.　According to the
same authority, the length of the Lepsa is 230 miles.　I have
preferred to follow Semeonoff, who himself visited the country
in 1856, and has collected all the most recent information
about it.

[4] *I. e.* 'variegated wood.'

[5] In 1864 the population had increased to 2589, nearly all of
whom were Cossacks.

The Lepsa, after leaving the valley of Chubar-agatch,[6] forces its way through the outer chain of the Alatau before entering the plain, where its course is N.N.W., and afterwards N.W. Here its banks are bordered by hillocks of drift-sand; and lower down by reeds, the haunt of the tiger (*Felis tigris*), being probably the northernmost limit of the distribution of this animal.

The Lepsa is about 170 miles long, 350 feet wide in its broadest part, and nine feet deep. Next to the Ili, it contains a greater volume of water than any of the rivers of this district. At Lepsinsky outpost a raft ferry crosses the river, on the high road from Ayaguz to Kopal.[7]

The Karatal (i. e. "black valley"), another of the seven rivers, has a longer course (200 miles), and is remarkable for the picturesque defile through which it rushes, after descending from the mountains in a series of leaps or cascades, the noise of which may be heard several versts off.

Its lower valley is clothed with luxuriant herbage, and is fertile in the extreme. Here it is

[6] Caravan roads to Kulja and Chuguchak pass through the Chubar-agatch Valley, where, according to Kirghiz traditions, the Khans of Dzungaria had their summer residence, and where an earthen mound or "Kurgan" still marks the place whence laws and justice were administered to their assembled subjects.

[7] This river has three sources—the Kara-tal, Chadji, and Kora, which take their rise in the snowy Alatau. It is afterwards joined by the Kok-su (blue water), which descends as a cascade from a gloomy chasm of the Alatau, and is broader and more rapid than the Kara-tal.

crossed by the high road from Kopal to Vernoye,
and lower still it again enters a narrow defile,
where the rocks are rudely carved to represent
various animals, such as deer, wild goat, &c.,
similar to the carvings on the banks of the
Yenissey. On emerging from this defile, the
Karatal, from a boisterous torrent, becomes a
tranquil steppe river, entering Lake Balkash by
three mouths, after a course from beginning to
end of 200 English miles, one-third of which is
among mountains and two-thirds through plains.
This river forms the boundary between the Great
and Middle Kirghiz hordes; on its banks are
numerous burial-grounds and graves, and amongst
these Buddhistic ruins of the seventeenth century.
We have already spoken of the Ayaguz, and as
the three smaller rivers, the Aksu, the Bien, and
the Koksu may be omitted in this brief sketch,
we will return to the lake itself and give some
account of the expedition sent to survey it in
1851.

The party was commanded by Lieut. Nifantieff,
and comprised two topographers, and a force of
seventy-six Cossacks. Early in spring preparations were commenced by building two boats at
Lepsa outpost, and launching them the first
favourable opportunity on the lake of that name.
The timber required for the purpose had to be
carried on camels' backs a distance of sixty miles,
the iron came from Omsk and Semipalatinsk, and

the anchors from the Irbit fair. All these preparations took up so much time, that it was the
beginning of August before a start could be
made. In the meantime, the water in the river
had fallen so low, that Nifantieff, fearing to over-
load the boats, decided on sending two months'
supplies and all the baggage by land on camels,
guarded by a convoy of Cossacks. The passage
of the boats down the river was a troublesome
matter, owing to the shallowness of the water.
Sand-banks were of constant occurrence, and the
boats had to be dragged over these by manual
labour, so that the expedition did not reach the
mouth of the Lepsa before the middle of August;
and here another difficulty had to be encountered.
Instead of flowing into the lake, as it was
supposed, the river disappeared in tall, thick
reeds and rushes two versts from it. Nifantieff
therefore determined on digging a trench two
versts long and ten feet wide, along the old
desiccated river-bed. After the work had pro-
gressed five days, it was found possible to flood
the trench from the river, but the depth of water
was insufficient to float the boats. Undaunted
by this new obstacle, Nifantieff constructed a
movable dam, of the felt coverings of two yurtas
or tents belonging to the party, and in this way
succeeded in raising the level of the water, and
floating his vessels; as these advanced the dam
was moved forward. This original device cost

superhuman efforts, but delay was out of the
question, and it was necessary to make the best
use of anything that came to hand. The last
impediment having been thus overcome, the expedition reached Lake Balkash. Here it was found
that the boats required repairing, and for this
purpose Nifantieff took them to the estuary of the
Ak-su, where the shore is sandy and they could
be hauled up, and again put in order. This done,
he sent one of his subordinates, Bulatoff, with a
party in one boat to Cape Chaukkar, with orders
to survey the northern shore from the cape to the
Ayaguz; whilst he himself put off in the other to
take soundings, and test the accuracy of previous
surveys along the southern shore, from the
Ayaguz to the Ak-su. A third party was instructed to continue the survey from the Ak-su to
the Kara-tal, and explore both these rivers for
fifty versts up-stream. A violent storm prevented
Bulatoff from accomplishing his task. Off the
promontory of Chaukkar he fell in with a current
which carried him towards the mouth of the
Lepsa. Anxious to meet his commanding officer,
who had already started for the mouth of the
Ayaguz, he coasted along the southern shore in
an easterly direction; but was shipwrecked off
the rocky cape of Aulieta, where, owing to the
violence of the gale, his cables parted, his anchor
was lost, and his boat cast ashore. In this plight
he decided on sending the boat with the Cossacks

to the mouth of the Ak-su for repairs, whilst he pushed on by land to the Ayaguz; hence he surveyed the northern shore as far as Cape Chaukkar.

Nifantieff's voyage was not altogether successful. He certainly accomplished a survey of the southern shore; but, on returning, his boat sustained considerable damage, owing to stress of weather. All these misadventures decided him on postponing further operations till the following year, particularly as the Cossacks had continually suffered from sea-sickness. On the 20th of September the boats were laid up for the winter at the mouth of the Ak-su, and Nifantieff, taking the anchors, ropes, and sails with him, returned to Kopal.

We will not follow him in his second year's explorations—suffice it to say, that in spite of great difficulties and hardships, the survey of the south-eastern shore of the lake and the delta of the Ili was completed, and the navigability of the lake ascertained.

One great difficulty attending the navigation of Lake Balkash is caused by the many rocky peninsulas which project far into the lake, especially on the north-west and west, and these, from the sunken rocks by which they are beset, are almost unapproachable in bad weather; the southern shores are low, overgrown with reeds, and extremely shallow.

Fogs are of rare occurrence, and then only in autumn, and are not dense enough to obstruct the navigation; but storms are violent and frequent, although not of long duration. The lake freezes over in the end of November or towards the middle of December, opening again in March. The ice is of no great thickness, but sufficiently strong to bear the ordinary winter traffic. The future importance of the lake depends in a great measure on the navigability of the river Ili; for when the districts round Kulja, which have so recently been the scenes of the most horrible bloodshed and desolation, are restored to a new life, a great deal of the traffic with Western China will pass this way, and Lake Balkash and the Ili may then become a great artery for the communications between the north-west and south-east.

LAKE ALA-KUL.

Humboldt's theory on the lake—Topography—Meaning of the name—Geographical position and height—Alternation in level—Rivers flowing into it—Subsidiary lakes ; Sassik-kul, or 'the stinking lake ;' Jélanash-kul, or 'the open lake '—Island of Aral-tiube—Russian settlement—Fate of Chuguchak—New Russo-Chinese trade-route—Ala-kul in summer—Barlyk range—Russo-Chinese frontier—Arasan, or mineral springs—The Ehbi wind—Legend concerning it—Inhabitants.

NEXT to Lake Balkash, and until comparatively recent times connected with it, is Lake Ala-kul, or, more correctly, Alak-kul, well known through the writings of Humboldt as the supposed centre of the volcanic forces of Central Asia until Schrenck personally visited it and found no trace of eruptive rocks either on the islands or round the lake. Lake Ala-kul is not easily mistaken, for it is the third largest lake as you travel east from the Caspian, the Aral coming first, Lake Balkash second, and then Ala-kul.[1]

A belt of desert marked with desiccated lake-beds and sand-waves, about sixty miles in extent,

[1] Issyk-kul, of much greater extent, lies several degrees farther south.

separates Lakes Ala-kul and Balkash, although, as we have said, they were united at no very distant period, Ala-kul now, however, is an entirely distinct basin.[2]

Three ranges pour their streams into it; on the north rises Tarbagatai, separated from the lake by a wide and thickly inhabited valley, on the east towers the Barlyk range, and on the south-west Ala-tau. The angle formed by these mountains contains the bulk of its water, whilst towards the west the level country is flooded for many miles in the direction of Balkash; and on the south a row of small lakes links it with Jélanash-kul, whence a narrow valley dividing Barlyk from Ala-tau leads to the Mongolian steppe.

At the present day Ala-kul consists of three lakes known under the general name of Ala-kul or "spotted lake," though some think that this name is, strictlly speaking, only applicable to the easternmost and largest of the three, whose water has a briny flavour, the centre one being called Urgali, and the westernmost Sassik-kul. The northern Tartars, with their guttural accent, pronounce it Ala-gul. On the Chinese, and many maps copied from them, the Kalmuk name Alak-tugul-nor, or "lake of the spotted

---

[2] Friar Rubruquis, who travelled through this country in 1254, apparently mistook Ala-kul for a part of Lake Balkash, but his topography is somewhat difficult to identify. See Schuyler's *Turkistan*, i. 402, *et seqq.*

bull," is given to it. But the Kalmuks now living in its vicinity do not recognize this name, and call it Ala-kul, as do also the Kirghiz and Russians. A great many of the topographical features of the country have been renamed by the Kirghiz as they spread over this region, but the most important about which they had heard before they came preserved their old names. For instance, they had heard of the river Ili before they occupied its banks, and its name was therefore retained. The new Kirghiz names are generally borrowed from some characteristic feature, hence it is always interesting to inquire into the etymology of these words.

It is evident, as M. Semeonoff remarks, that the Kirghiz called Ala-kul "the spotted lake" because of its islands, to distinguish it from lakes Zaisan, Issyk-kul, and even Sassik-kul, which have no islands. The Kalmuk name is curious, but we find many such terms applied to mountains in the steppe, as, for instance Turaigir, i.e. spotted horse; and in the same way Alak-tugul (spotted bull) may probably refer to some mountain near the lake, or to one of its islands. Its ancient name was Gurgeh-nor, or lake of bridges, doubtless from the long, narrow promontories which extend far into the lake, and when its level was unusually low may have reached from shore to shore, and formed isthmuses of dry land or natural bridges.

Not very long ago an isthmus of this kind, now submerged in the centre, might have been seen. The geographical position of the lake was accurately fixed in 1862 by astronomical observations, and topographical surveys have since then been made of its shores by officers of the Siberian corps. Its approximate height above ocean level has been calculated to be about 780 feet, or very nearly that of Lake Balkash, whilst Lake Zaisan to the north-east is considerably higher.[*]　As we have said, Ala-kul now consists of three lakes, but these were doubtless formerly united in one, and are so represented by the Chinese maps, their authors probably never having heard of more than one lake.　The appearance of the sands, the shores here and there rising in cliffs, bearing evident traces of having been once washed by the waves, which have now receded to some distance, and lastly the desiccated lake-beds, all indicate unmistakably a former higher level of its waters.

[*] The question of the height of Lakes Ala-kul and Balkash has been the subject of some geographical controversy.　Golubieff, from whose account of Ala-kul I have borrowed these particulars, estimates Ala-kul to be 1200 feet above the sea, Balkash between 900 and 1200, whilst he gives 1900 as the height of the town of Chuguchak　Semeonoff, however, shows that Balkash cannot be more than 780 feet, and that Ala-kul lies considerably below Zaisan, whose height is generally admitted to be 1300 feet.　If we consider the difficulty of determining heights in the heart of the continent, and the delicate instruments required for this purpose, we may leave a wide margin for possible errors.

Schrenk, who visited it in 1832, noticed two smaller lakes of recent formation immediately to the south, showing that its water had recently subsided.

The Kirghiz are comparatively new comers, and have no traditions of the former union of the lakes, but their testimony as to the changes which Ala-kul has undergone since they knew it is interesting, for they assert that its level was formerly considerably higher, and that their fore-fathers remember the time when the northern shore was submerged for a distance of nearly 1800 feet beyond the present water-mark. It then fell, and twenty-seven years ago stood so low that small islands, now 200 yards from the mainland, came to be united with it. Ever since it has been gradually rising, as may be seen by the isthmuses of Uzunai and Naryn-uzak, where some years ago Kirghiz and caravans encamped and crossed, but which are now partially under water.

The neighbouring mountains supply an abundance of water to the lake. The most important of the streams joining it is the Imel or Emil, which in spring swells to the size of a torrent, and hurls great boulders down to the valley, tearing up trees of great age growing along its upper course, and stranding them in the valley below, to the great profit of the inhabitants. At all other seasons of the year the streams are fordable, and even the Imel, where it is crossed by the caravan road, is in the month of August only seventy feet wide.

All these little rivers form small lakes at their estuaries, thickly overgrown with reeds, which cover a vast area to the south of Sassik-kul, and form a belt along its northern shore. In spring these swamps are inundated, and the subsiding water leaves large stagnant pools, which in summer exhale unwholesome miasma, whence the lake derives its name Sassik-kul, i. e. "stinking or suffocating lake."

For a distance of twenty versts from the southern extremity of Ala-kul, extends a belt of small lakes, formed by a few mountain streams, and terminating in Jélanash-kul, which must not be omitted in this notice. This lake is small, six miles long, by two and a half wide, with bitter but hardly saline water. Its name signifies "open lake," because it is exposed to view on all sides.

Jélanash-kul has no communication with Ala-kul, and is separated from the chain of small lakes forming a continuation with the latter by a narrow stony ridge, Tash-kala, consisting of gravel and pebbles, and formed by the action of the waves raised by the wind, which blows for the greater part of the year in the direction of Ala-kul. The waves have piled up a regular embankment of small pebbles which is continually increasing; ever working in one direction, and obedient to the laws of mechanics, it has imparted a curve to this natural breakwater, like that given by engineers to moles and jetties. The isthmus of Naryn-uzak, now submerged, was formed in the same way, and of similar substances. From the waters of Ala-kul rises the rocky cone of Aral-tiube, which had once a great reputation as an active volcano of the central continent. Humboldt supposed it to be so, no less from the accounts received from the Tartars, as from his own belief in the existence of volcanoes in the heart of Asia.[4]

Near Aral-tiube is a second small island, and some versts to the north a rock rises straight up from the water connected with the shore by a narrow neck of sand. When the level of Ala-kul was higher, the isthmus was submerged, and the rock formed a third island, Baigazi-tiube. The summit of the first of these peaks is nearly 630 feet above the level of the lake. It may be seen from a considerable distance, and its dark solitary mass brooding over the green surface of the lake enhances the gloom of the desolate landscape.

Along the valley on the northern shore of Ala-kul the Russians long ago established relations with China. This was the point where the frontiers of the two empires were more closely joined than elsewhere.

[4] It is hardly necessary to remark that Humboldt's conclusions on volcanic phenomena in Central Asia have been remarkably confirmed by the late Dr. Stoliczka's researches north of Kashgar.—(See Rep. of a Mission to Yarkand, 1873, pp. 466—469.)

A Russian settlement was founded on the river Urdjar, which already contained in 1863 nearly two hundred houses, and had every prospect of becoming a flourishing place. Seventy miles to the E.S.E. of it was Chuguchak, numbering 10,000 houses [5] before the Mohammedan insurrection.

The valley is abundantly watered, and fertile. The inhabitants, Russians as well as Chinese, produce crops of corn and vegetables. Along the road from Urdjar to Chuguchak lie Kirghiz fields, and twenty versts before reaching the latter place are scattered Chinese farms, becoming more and more numerous every year as the population in-

[5] By the treaty of Kulja (1851), the Russians were allowed to establish a factory and to have agents at Chuguchak, and this town, owing to its geographical position, might have become an important depôt for the trade between Russia and China, had it not fallen in 1865 into the hands of the Mohammedan insurgents, and by them been reduced to ashes. Owing to the disturbed state of these frontier provinces a new trade-route had to be explored, and General Poltoratsky having pointed out the superior advantages of the line of the Black Irtysh and Buluntohoi (recently surveyed by Sosnoffsky), an enterprising firm of Moscow merchants organized in 1872 a large caravan to penetrate, by this way if possible, into China. From the account given by Morozoff's clerk or caravan bashi, communicated by Poltoratsky to the Geographical Society of St. Petersburg, it appears that they succeeded in selling most of their wares, but were turned back by the Chinese at Barkul. No subsequent attempts have, as far as I am aware, been made to develope this new Russo-Chinese trade-route; but it is not improbable that the establishment of a Chinese embassy at St. Petersburg, announced by the newspapers, may be the beginning of a new era of commercial intercourse between the two empires.

creases. Amongst these it is not unusual to see
in the midst of fields of vegetables variegated
plantations of poppy, beneath whose flowery
carpet lurks the future poison. Beyond these
farms lies Chuguchak in the midst of a smiling
landscape. But the climate is so severe that fruit-
trees cannot be successfully cultivated; water and
other melons, though grown in large quantities, are
of bad quality.

On approaching Ala-kul the soil becomes more
sterile at every step, sandy saline patches of soil
appear now entirely bare, now thinly covered
with sickly plants. The streams which descend
the mountains with bright limpid water, splashing
noisily in their rocky beds, expand into lakes, or
disappear imperceptibly, imparting their moisture
to the soil, and sustaining the thick growth of
reeds. The Kirghiz retreat to the mountains in
order to avoid the summer heats, and the silence
of the desert is unbroken by any sound. The
solitary traveller will in vain seek for signs of life,
and will only be deceived by the mirage. Per-
chance his attention may be attracted to a column
of smoke rising in the distance. "Shaitan Shalit!"
exclaims the Kirghiz, and the less superstitious
traveller knows it to be the tornado rising from
the sandy plains. The shores of Ala-kul in some
places bare, in others are covered with reeds, and
in summer swarm with water-fowl and mosquitoes.
On leaving Ala-kul you will long remember with

dread the tormenting little persecutors, and the
sharp metallic voices of swans and geese will long
ring in your ears.   Ala-tau and Barlyk approach
quite close to the lake.   The former is well known,
but the latter awaits its explorer.   Several of the
peaks are visible from the shore of the lake, the
highest of them, Ak-chek, being only 2800 feet
above sea-level.

In the spurs of both ranges are many valleys,
with excellent pasture and arable land, watered
by streams whose banks are fringed with Lonicera,
barberry, dog-rose, and clumps of poplars.

A line of Chinese outposts formerly passed along
the Barlyk range, marking the Russo-Chinese
frontier in the west.[6] Each of these consisted of

---

[6] This was the position of affairs when M. Golubieff wrote his
report (1863); but it is difficult to say what may be the actual
state of the frontier guards in the extreme west. Veniukoff, in
his review of the frontiers of Russia in Asia, says that the
treaty of Chuguchak (1864) was never fully carried out, probably owing to the outbreak in 1865 of the Dungan insurrection, and the Dzungarian section of the frontier, from Khan-
Tengri on the south to Khabar-assu on the north, remains prac-
tically undefined.   East of this again in the Altai-Sayan section,
he estimates the Chinese regular forces at 580 Manchus and
Chinese distributed in two towns situated 2000 versts (about
1300 miles) from the Great Wall, i. e. from the frontiers of China
proper. "From Kobdo and Uliassutai," he says, "we could drive
the Chinese out at any time, for their fortifications are so weak,
that in 1870 and 1872 bands of badly-armed insurgents had no
difficulty in taking them. But," he adds, "it is clearly our interest
not only *not* to molest the Chinese in this part of Central Asia;
but, on the contrary, to use every means in our power to consoli-
date their rule over the local nomads."   A glance at the map will

a few small houses, surrounded by yurtas, to accommodate the guard and their families, and the officer in charge, or galda; in the background stands a small temple.

The nomad Kalmuks in the neighbourhood supplied the guard. At the more important stations, such as Manitu on the Emil, and at Chagan-togai, they occupied themselves with husbandry, and bred sheep and cattle. But the poverty and dirt of these stations are very striking, as well as the naive, consequential air of the officers. The galda, on matter how ragged his dress, will not hesitate to hold ceremonious audiences, seated on a saddle for want of some other article of furniture.

Not far from Chagan-togai, and nearer Ala-kul, the warm mineral springs of Arassan[7] bubble up at the foot of a rock of porphyry. They are nearly 750 feet above the lake. There are two of them both containing sulphur, of the same kind as those at Kopal, but warmer, their temperature on issuing from the ground being 110° Fahr.

The Arassan springs appear to have been wor-

at once convince the reader, how unwise it would be for Russia to advance beyond the splendid natural frontier afforded by the mountain ranges of south-western Siberia, into the steppes and deserts on the south.

[7] This appears to be the word used by the natives for springs in general. Schuyler says that numerous warm springs of a medicinal character, called *arasan*, are found to the west and south-west of Sairam-nor.

shipped by the Kalmuks, who have built near them
a small shrine, in which are to be seen painted
images. But the Kalmuks, driven out by the
Kirghiz, have retired from here, and the springs
which they formerly visited have fallen into the
hands of their late rivals, and especially the
Tartars, who bring their women hither to be cured
of barrenness.

In 1862 meteorological observations were commenced at the Russian factory at Chuguchak, but
as this town a few years later fell into the hands
of the Dungans and their Kirghiz allies, it is
impossible to look for important scientific data
from this direction.

The shores of Ala-kul are remarkable for
the sultriness of the summer heat, and at this
period of the year they are uninhabitable. The
Kirghiz seek pasturage for their cattle, and a
cooler climate in the mountains, only descending
again in August to fix their winter encampments
round Ala-kul, where they find convenient shelter
for their tents and herds. In October the first
snow falls, in November Ala-kul freezes up, and
does not thaw again before April.

On the northern shore of the lake, where the
population is sedentary, the summer heat is not
great, and the frost not severe, though the thermometer often falls to 13° Fahr. The S.E. wind
called Ehbi (Yubi), blows from autumn till April,
through the narrow defile separating Ala-tau from

the Barlyk range, leading out on to Lake Kyzyl-tuz or Balkatsi-nor. This wind blows from regions bare of snow, and is so violent at times as to have the force of a hurricane, raising clouds of snow and dust, and putting a stop to all communications. Solitary travellers have been known to perish during one of these wind-storms, and be covered up in the snow, and it is said whole villages have been buried in this way. Caravans bound for Kulja are afraid of it, and always wait till it is over, or prefer the road through the mountains, rather than keep to the level, and expose themselves to its fury.[s] The Ehbi wind is warm and dry, probably because it blows across snowless tracts. The Kirghiz and Tartars have a legend that this wind issues from some caverns which the Kalmuks have in vain tried to fill up with stones; every time they make the attempt the wind blows the stones aside, and bursts forth with renewed strength. They place these caverns somewhere between Ala-tau and Barlyk, but the nearer one gets to these mountains the more misty and fanciful are the stories told of them, so that they are doubtless as much the work of imagination as the legends of volcanic eruption of Aral-tiube. The

[s] Schuyler says that when this wind blows through the defile, it is felt at Sergiopol, 250 miles off, and that M. Zakharoff, in passing through it, was immediately obliged to leave the main road, and take a steeper path through the mountains.— *Turkistan,* ii. 191.

natural explanation of the Ehbi is the prevalence of the east wind in winter, which, checked in its progress by the mountains, bursts through the narrow defile into the steppes of Ala-kul.

In the ravine of Altyn Immel (200 miles to the south-west of Ala-kul) a similar wind blows in winter, also called Ehbi, by the Kirghiz. It clears away the snow from the Ili valley, thus rendering it habitable for the nomads in winter.

It only remains to add a few words on the actual inhabitants of the lake shores. These at the end of the last century were Kalmuks (Dzungars). At Chugutsa, near the Urdjar of to-day, the last of their Khans, Amursana, formed his camp.

When the Kalmuks were subjugated in Kienlong's time, the Chinese founded the town of Chuguchak at this spot. But the site proved to be unfavourable, owing to its dampness, and it was soon removed to its present position.

The Chinese, exasperated by their long wars, and determined to rid themselves for ever of so dangerous an enemy, did not spare the Kalmuks. They were slain nearly to a man, only a few saving themselves by flight. In this way the steppes of Ala-kul and the valleys of the neighbouring mountains were entirely depopulated, but not for long, and the Kirghiz coming from the west soon occupied the free lands.

At the present day the Kirghiz of the Middle Horde inhabit the country round the lake. Its southern shores, together with the neighbouring valleys of the Ala-tau and Barlyk ranges, are occupied by Kizais, whilst to their north and to the east of the lake, along the valley of the Emil and the slopes of the Tarbagatai, are encamped the Tumentsi.

All these tribes are included in the Sergiopol district of the Semipalatinsk region.[9]

[9] The above particulars of Lake Ala-kul are for the most part borrowed from an article by the late M. Golubieff, of the Imperial Russian staff corps, who commanded a surveying party sent in 1859, to explore this part of Asia; and the article on Lake Balkash from a paper by General Babkoff, of the same corps, who directed the topographical survey of that lake in 1864.

THE STAROVERTSI.

As Colonel Prejevalsky has alluded in his travels
to the " Starovertsi," or Old Believers, and their

visit to Lake Lob, it may not be out of place
here to give a short account of these much
persecuted people. It is hardly necessary to
remind the reader of their origin, suffice it to
say that when the patriarch Nikon introduced
his reforms and innovations into Russia in the
time of Peter the Great, a large body of the
clergy and laity refused to abide by them, and
remained strict adherents to the religion of their
ancestors. Hence arose the *raskol* or split in the
National Church, which has been described by
Dean Stanley, Mouravieff, Dr. Neale, Wallace, and
others.

I myself came across some of the Starovertsi
when staying nearly twenty years ago in a small
town in one of the central provinces of Russia.
My acquaintances there belonged chiefly to the
mercantile class, and it is in their midst that the
spirit of conservatism in religious matters is so
strong. I was on visiting terms with two families,
the one representing the old sectarian clique with
its clinging attachment to the habits, customs, and
dress of bygone days, the other belonging to the
progressive party of modern Russia. The head of
the former, by name Evgraf Vassilievitch B——,
was a man between sixty and seventy, he wore
the long black frock-coat of a former generation,
and his white beard added dignity to a handsome
and expressive countenance; though undoubtedly
a Starover, he showed no signs of dissent from the

orthodox Church, and even filled the official position
of mayor of the town, but he neither smoked, nor
drank wine, nor played cards, and the women of
his family led a life of complete seclusion. Once,
however, when dining at his house, I was honoured
by an introduction to his wife and daughter; the
latter was of a delicate refined beauty such as may
be met with in many an English home, and her
charms were well set off by the Kokoshka, or high
head-dress with the long veil falling behind, for
which the women of these districts are remarkable.
Evgraf Vassilievitch spoke but little, this however
might have been accounted for by my then imper-
fect knowledge of the Russian language. Among
the books that he lent me was the best known standard novel of the day " Yuri Miloslafsky," written
much in the same style as Walter Scott's novels,
and another work in modern Greek. The other
family I visited was of quite a different stamp. M.
Obrastsoff was a well-to-do, prosperous merchant
who in dress and appearance followed the fashions
of the day, he kept open house once a week, to
which all were made welcome, and his daughter,
very gay and pretty, played quadrilles and smoked
cigarettes. His two sons assisted their father in
the mornings at the pristan or wharf, where stood
his warehouse, in which was stored the flax that he
bought during the winter, and shipped in spring
for St. Petersburg. In the afternoon they either
amused themselves by driving their fast-trotting

horses in light racing-sledges, or joining the
wealth and aristocracy of the place at the *gulánia*
or promenade, a very solemn affair, where every
one in their showiest equipage, paraded at foot's
pace round and round the solitary square in the
little town.   M. Obrastsoff once showed me a medal
he had received for services rendered to the
Government in the reign of the Emperor Nicholas
in assisting the police to apprehend some of the
Starovertsi, a work he said of considerable difficulty, and some personal risk, for in those days
they were very numerous, and often offered a
determined resistance to the authorities.   Their
spirit and organization, however, were at last completely broken by the stringent measures taken
against them; the few who still refused to submit
left their homes and sought refuge in all sorts of
out-of-the-way nooks and corners, but generally
on the very outskirts of the vast empire, where
they were beyond the interference of the police,
and were allowed the free and unrestrained
exercise of their religion.   The Governments of
Archangel and Olonetz have always been their
great haven of refuge, and in the midst of the
almost inaccessible tundras or bogs, they built
convents, monasteries, and churches which were
secretly supported by their wealthy brethren at
Moscow and St. Petersburg.   Some of these
remained till within the last twenty or thirty
years, and, for aught I know to the contrary, may

exist still; but the backbone of dissent was broken
in the reign of Nicholas. Many of the *pomortsi*,
or owners of coasting vessels on the shores of the
White Sea, in the Gulf of Onega, and towards
Kem and Kola, when I lived among them, were
Starovertsi. Their vessels, mostly lugger-rigged,
and a few schooners, were named after their
patron saints, on whom they placed such implicit
reliance that it was the exception to find any
nautical instrument, or even a compass among
them.

What the particular sect of the Starovertsi
were who visited Lob-nor [1] Colonel Prejevalsky

---

[1] Grigorieff suggests that these fishermen on Lake Lob are not
only *not* the remnants of the aborigines, but new comers of
quite a recent date—probably not before the end of the seventeenth century, and very closely related to the Russians, in
fact, none other than the *Staro-obriadtsi*, who had made their
way thither from Southern Siberia. Indeed reports to this
effect were current in the last-named country. If this be the
case, continues Grigorieff in his note to the Russian edition
of *Ritter's Asia*, the dislike of these fishermen to meat and
bread is easily explained—not that they cannot digest such
food, but that when they happen to visit Korla on fast-days,
which are of frequent occurrence in the Greek Church, they
could on no account touch meat or wheaten cakes made with
butter, and would show their disgust of such food if they
chanced to swallow some of it unawares. From Prejevalsky's
narrative we glean that this is not the case, the population on
the Tarim and Lake Lob being described as a curious mixture of
refugees from all parts of Turkestan, including Sarts, Kirghiz,
and Tangutans. That Starovertsi have recently visited Lake
Lob is however evident, from the account given by the natives
to Prejevalsky of the sudden appearance of this people.

does not tell us, but an interesting account is given by a traveller, Mr. Printz, of a visit in 1863 to the *Kamenshiki*, of the Bukhtarminsk volost of the Government of Tomsk, from which we extract the following :—

After the year 1747 when the Government took over from Demidoff the mines and works in the Altai, many new settlements were founded in the mountains, and the whole district received the official name of Kolyvano-Voskresensk, after the first mines opened there.

The boundaries of this new district were defined, and the Empress Elizabeth, on sending Brigadier-General Beer there in 1747, bade him take possession in the name of H.I.M. of the Kolyvano-Voskresensky, Barnaoul, and Shulbin works, together with all the land, mechanics, and peasants belonging to them. He was further directed to construct a chain of forts to protect the works and mines from the inroads of the Kalmuks of Dzungaria. In 1759 the lines of Kolyvan and Kuznetsk were completed, and formed the boundary of the empire from Ust-Kamennogorsk to Kuznetsk; this was called "the old line." But as the mining industry developed, miners and settlers soon crossed this frontier, so that by 1764 a second line had to be laid down in a south-easterly direction, entering the mountains at Tegeretsky outpost and Fort Verkhny Charish, whence it continued in a north and north-easterly direction to the town of Kuznetsk. South of Tegeretsk the line passed as before to Ust-Kamennogorsk on the Irtysh, whence it was, however, subsequently advanced up the Bukhtarma. Before the Kuznetsk and Kolyvan lines were drawn, the districts included by them were called "Bielovodiye." Many of the inhabitants of north-western Russia made their way hither in numbers following on the tracks of the trapper and hunter, some to rid themselves of the burdens and duties imposed upon them by the state, others to escape punishment, all to seek a free life, to trade with the natives, and hunt wild animals, unburdened by taxes, and unshackled by official inspection. In order to secure themselves against the attacks of Tartars and Kalmuks they founded their first settlements in the dense impassable forests of the present district of Kuznetsk, where those of their number who adhered to the old belief made for themselves caves (*skiti*) and hermitages. This took place between 1719 and 1723. As soon as the Kolyvan-Kuznetsk frontier was adopted, and the country parcelled out into districts, the whole of this region lost its reputation as a free land, and the hermitages and "retreats" became in course of time villages. All or most of those who had migrated hither, including persons of every rank and station in life, and who were called *prishelsti*, or immigrants, were included in the third general census (1764), and were made liable to work in the mines and Government works. Hence the term " Bielovodiye," came to be henceforward applied to those uninhabited districts lying beyond the Kolyvan-Kuznetsk frontier line in a south-easterly direction towards China. This country was entirely uninhabited, yet it abounded in all the requirements of life, and could serve as a refuge for all who sought concealment. To this new " Bielovodiye" to "the rock," Starovertsi of all classes and conditions began to flock. Here they were unmolested and feared no pursuit, here they were at liberty to exercise the rights of their religious belief.

These dissenters were soon joined by others who belonged to no particular sect, but were for the most part runaway operatives from the works, and persons of every class who wished to escape from labour and taxation. Among them in more recent times were emigrants from distant parts of the empire, from the Government of Archangel, Skiti, or cave-dwellers, from the Government of Olonetz and the forests of Solikama, &c.

To this day there are ravines in the Altai mountains called " Kamen" (rock), and their inhabitants are usually spoken of as people living " in the rock," or " beyond the rock," whence their name of *Kamenshiki*, or " people of the rock." Their first settlement, tradition has it, was com-composed of only four men, who retired " to the rock" from religious motives, and founded their

P

habitation upwards of a century ago on the river
Ulba beyond the Holsun range. But when one
of their number had been caught, and their
retreat discovered, the others, fearful lest a
similar fate might await them, retired to the
inhospitable and lonely gorges of the Bukhtarma
range. But here, whether the gregarious instinct
of their nature was too strong for them, or
whether impelled by hunger, they did not long lie
hid. By degrees they began to show themselves
in the nearest Russian settlements, and especially
in those whose inhabitants were more favourably
disposed towards the *raskol*, or "dissent." Their
holiness and humility, real or feigned, attracted
the inhabitants towards them, and by depicting
their " retreat " in as favourable a light as possible
they succeeded in persuading others to flee with
them to their home in the mountains. In the
course of a short time a good many, mostly
peasants, made their way thither, having obtained
leave from the authorities to absent themselves
for the avowed object of hunting, and then
remaining away for good and all.

These " kamenshiki," anxious to avoid all pursuit, took up their abode in the most inaccessible
ravines of the Listviajny range, along the right
tributaries of the Bukhtarma, near the sources of
the Katuna, Kok-su, and other rivers. They built
their huts in the midst of wild scenery, combining,
however, a few advantages for their domestic

cattle, and for agricultural purposes, surrounded
on all sides by grand mountains and well-watered
streams. They lived peaceably together observing
strictly the rites of their religion. The virgin soil
bountifully repaid their agricultural labours, and
the skins of wild beasts were a source of untold
wealth to the hunters. In short they could enjoy
a free and independent life. Fugitives usually
started for "the rock" in spring, and on arriving
there, if they had time, built themselves log-huts
or shanties, or sometimes stayed with others
already settled there, helping them with their
household work, sowing the corn, mowing the
hay, or attending to the fisheries. On the
approach of autumn, the best season for hunting
the fur animals, they would go on hunting
expeditions.

In the hunting districts, more or less distant
from their homes, the Kamenshiki built themselves rude huts in which they passed the winter
occupied during the whole of the time in trapping
wild animals. These huts were of the rudest kind,
care being always taken, however, that one corner
should be over a spring, in order to obtain water
without going outside for it, a precaution always
adopted to avoid the labour of keeping an opening
clear in the ice to some spring. The huts of these
trappers were often completely buried in snow-
drifts several yards deep, and a small opening was
all that marked the entrance. The only faint

signs of life in these snowy wastes and dense
forests, were the stack of firewood, the black bath,
and the *saira*, or larder, supported on four trees
standing close together, cut off about fifteen feet
from ground so as to leave posts on which a few
boards were laid, and a sloping roof constructed.
In this way they would pass the whole winter
engaged in hunting, returning home in spring,
when every man brought back his twenty sable
and one hundred squirrel skins, to say nothing of
other kinds. Besides these winter occupations
the Kamenshiki would occasionally make expeditions to the river Irtysh in small parties of eight,
leaving one of their number behind to attend to
the house. On reaching the Irtysh they would
halt somewhere near the mouth of the Bukhtarma,
whence they would ascend to the Narym, a right
tributary of the Irtysh. Here the first thing was
to build themselves canoes, and then set traps for
the sturgeon and sterlet, which they dried on the
spot, or jerked in the sun, to facilitate transport,
and preserve it from spoiling. These fishing
expeditions would sometimes be so successful that
they would obtain enough to load ten horses,
which were expressly sent for at the close of the
season.

Sometimes, too, small parties of them would
proceed from the Bukhtarma to the fisheries on
Lake Zaisan, out of which the Irtysh flows.
Ascending this river, they would have to run the

gauntlet of the cordon of Chinese pickets, where, in order to escape observation, they always travelled at night-time. Arrived at the lake, they followed its right shore to the estuary of the Upper or Black Irtysh, to which they gave the name of "sluggish," and proceeded up its stream for some twenty or thirty miles. Selecting the most convenient spots, they built earthen huts, and pursued their fishing and trapping avocations unmolested by any one. They hunted the beaver and the otter, extracting from the former when skinned the valuable *castoreum*, which they salted to prevent its spoiling, and afterwards sold to Tashkend and Chinese merchants, who came to them for this purpose from the aouls or Kirghiz encampments, and the left bank of the Irtysh.

One pressing want of the Kamenshiki was salt, and this was supplied partly by the Kirghiz-Kazaks, and partly by digging it themselves out of the salt lakes on the steppe, about thirty miles from the Loktieff works. The difficulty of obtaining it from the lacustrine salt-beds was very great, and attended by considerable risk, the greatest precautions being necessary in going thither to escape notice on the road. Taking a sufficient supply of provisions, the Kamenshiki would issue from the mountains, riding always by night, and halting by day in some unfrequented spot. The salt they collected in the lakes was put into bags slung on either side of their horses, and they returned home in the same stealthy manner. They procured their domestic cattle, cows and sheep, from the Kirghiz-Kazaks nomadizing on the right bank of the Irtysh, between the rivers Bukhtarma and Narym.

Many of the Kamenshiki, having been employed in the Government works in various capacities, would now and then invite their friends and relations to a rendezvous, taking care that it should be at a respectful distance from their settlement, notwithstanding which they were frequently captured by the authorities.

The Government, although aware of the colony of outlaws in the Bukhtarma district, was unable to take any effectual measures against them, owing to the inaccessible and unknown country in which they lived, and because, sensible of the danger they always ran of being discovered, the Kamenshiki continued to retire farther and farther into the wildest and most unapproachable recesses of the mountains. The first time we hear of their being discovered was in 1761, on the river Turgun-ussu, when Lieutenant Zeleony, commanding a company of soldiers and mining officials to explore new sites for settlements on the Upper Bukhtarma, found in a ravine a small hut with two Russians living in it, whom, however, he did not succeed in capturing. The first detailed accounts of the domestic life, occupations, and industry of these people reached the Government in 1791, soon after

the Imperial pardon had been granted them in an
ukàz addressed to General Peel, acting-governor-
general of the principalities of Irkutsk and Kolyvan, when they were made liable to a small poll-
tax, and later to tribute in kind (*Yassak*).   In the
early stage of the existence of the Kamenshiki,
when their number was but small, and they were
for the most part devotees, their lives were
patriarchal in the extreme, and having cut themselves off from the world, united by a common lot,
they formed a religious brotherhood or community,
living together in peace and harmony.   They had
no serious disagreements, but when any misunder-
standing or dispute arose among them, the case was
referred to their "best men," those who possessed
the confidence of the whole body, and were distinguished above their fellows for their moral
qualities.   The decision of these men, which was
given verbally, was considered final, and held the
place of law.   But when reports of the free life led
by these people had induced many to join who
were chiefly deserters, operatives from the works,
criminals punished and unpunished, and others of
the same class, their numbers increased, and in
equal proportion every kind of wickedness to
which unbridled licence could lead.   Women were
violated, robberies, and even murders were com-
mitted.   Owing to the preponderance of men, the
want of the other sex was greatly felt, and became
the chief cause of discord.   Wives and daughters

were abducted, and strife and crime took the place
of peace and goodwill.   Criminals went unpunished
or fell victims to the revenge of the injured party.
Their morals grew lax, more particularly owing to
the absence of the refining influences of religion.
Far removed from churches and clergy, the
Kamenshiki neglected all religious observances,
and partook of no sacraments.   Matters at last
became so bad that the very mode of dealing with
the most turbulent spirits displayed the greatest
severity.   It is related how once, in 1788, some of
their number caught in the commission of crime
were unanimously sentenced to the following
extraordinary punishment: two of the criminals
were bound to small rafts, and set adrift in the
rapid Bukhtarma; each had a pole given him to
save himself from drowning, and a loaf of bread
for food.   In this way the community, finding it
impossible to keep two such miscreants in their
midst, and unwilling to execute capital punishment on them, determined to get rid of them by
leaving blind fate to decide whether they should
live or die; one was drowned, the other was
washed on to the bank.   But as this example did
not have the desired effect of restoring order, the
ringleaders and some of their confederates were
seized and condemned to die.   A mere accident
saved their lives.   One of the Kamenshiki happened to shoot a Chinese military officer, who,
enraged at the occurrence, came to demand that

justice should be done him; finding the people
assembled and about to execute their prisoners, he
bade his soldiers surround them, and insisted on
the release of the doomed men.

This was not the only occasion that the Kamenshiki came into contact with the Chinese. They
frequently attacked the Kirghiz beyond the Irtysh,
who were not slow to revenge themselves by
plundering the Kamenshiki. Both sides had recourse to the interference of the Chinese, whose
arbitration never carried much weight.

The internal discords of the Kamenshiki, and
the inefficacy of the measures taken by them to
restore order caused many to think of more certain
means of safety. A succession of bad harvests
for three years was an additional incentive to
abandon resorts which had grown terrible to them,
and return to their former homes, but the dread
of the punishment which they had incurred
deterred them. At length they decided to place
themselves under the protection of the Chinese
Government. Accordingly sixty of their families
assembled, and proceeded to the Chinese frontier
guard-house of Jinghiz-tai, twenty-three miles
from the present village of Fikalka. Halting at a
little distance from the guard-house, they deputed
six of their number to communicate with the noyen,
or frontier official, and learn his wishes, but as
their envoys did not return, the remainder waited
no longer, but threw themselves, their wives, and

children, on the mercy of the noyen.   On arriving
at the guard-house of Jinghiz-tai, they were at
.once sent forward under an escort to Kobdo, the
chief town of the border province of the same
name.   Here they were presented to the governor,
who interrogated them, and gave orders to place
them all together in some building, a kind of
barrack, or more probably gaol, where they were
kept some time under strict surveillance, receiving
however, enough to live upon.   At length they
were set at liberty, and informed that a message
had been received from Peking, to say that the
Emperor of China would not receive them among
his subjects, but in consideration of their poverty
ordered that a supply of food should be given them
for the road, and that they should be sent to the
place whence they had come.   They were accordingly taken back in the same way, and by the same
route.   Riding horses were given them, and means
of subsistence.   They were delighted at receiving
their liberty again, for the frequent executions
they had witnessed during their captivity, even for
the most trivial offences, gave them a bad impression of the Chinese people and Government.

After their return, although the Chinese frontier
officials protected them whenever they had recourse
to their assistance, both against their own fellows
as well as the neighbouring Kirghiz, yet this did
not ·put a stop to internal dissensions, and the
fear of being caught and punished was a constant

source of uneasiness to them.   These fears were
not groundless, for the Russian Government had
from time to time taken measures against the
Kamenshiki.   Cossack patrols had been sent into
the mountains from the nearest fortresses, and
though these had hitherto confined their operations
to setting fire to some dwellings, and surprising and
making prisoners of a few stray members of the
community, yet the Kamenshiki lived in constant
dread of pursuit, and the visits of parties of miners
kept them continually on the *qui-vive*, and at
length induced them to surrender themselves to
the Government.   At a meeting held in 1788 it
was proposed to select one of their body as a
deputy, and authorize him to ask pardon of the
Government, and permission to remain in their
present place of abode on payment of tribute or
some tax.   This resolution, however, was not then
carried, in consequence of the opposition of some
of the elders or " best men," who feared being compelled to renounce their rock, and return to their
former mode of life.

When mining operations were begun in the district of Bukhtarma, officials were sent with detach-
ments of soldiers and labourers to explore and
work the new mines.   In 1790 the mining-over-
seer, Priyésjeff, and his assistant, left Fort Ust-
Kamennogorsk with twenty-four workmen and an
escort of Cossacks.   In the autumn, after the preliminary works had been completed, and most of

the escort had returned to the fortress, eleven armed men appeared one night at the station, who, on being challenged by the sentry, announced that they were hunters, and had come to see the overseer. Upon Priyésjeff coming out to them, one of their number, Ivan Buikoff, a runaway dragoon, speaking on behalf of himself and his comrades, said that he and three hundred able-bodied and armed companions were ready to give in their submission to the Government, and perform any service required of them.

Priyésjeff immediately communicated this to the authorities of the mining department, who referred it to the Empress Catherine II. The allegiance of the Kamenshiki was accepted, and the Imperial answer given in an ukàz dated the 15th September, 1791, and addressed to General Peel, Governor of Siberia.

According to information furnished at that time to those in power, the Kamenshiki numbered three hundred and eighteen, of whom two hundred and eighteen were men, and sixty-eight women; that they were in reality more numerous was admitted by their own delegates, who said that the absence of many on hunting and fishing expeditions rendered the return incomplete. They occupied thirty settlements, and comprised chiefly peasants, foot-soldiers, dragoons, and operatives, Cossacks of the line, and a few domestic serfs, refugees from the hermitages and caves of the Starovertsi in the governments of European Russia, only four out of the whole number were escaped convicts.

The Imperial pardon put an end to all disorder among the Kamenshiki, and established order and harmony : they abandoned their terrible cliffs and ravines, silent witnesses of the crimes and irregularities of their past lives, and removed to localities offering every possible advantage for tillage, cattle-breeding, and industrial pursuits.   In nearly every settlement they built houses of prayer, but no church, as the inhabitants were Starovertsi, or Old Believers.   A few of the elders and book-men, chosen from their midst, fulfilled all sacred duties, and conducted the service, recourse being had to the fortress only for the celebration of weddings. But in the course of time this was all changed, many of the inhabitants, fearing lest they should be included in the number of those liable to compulsory labour in the works, left of their own accord for other villages, crown peasants took their places, and the very names of the settlements were altered.

Fifteen years ago the descendants of the Kamen-shiki inhabited besides the district of Bukhtarma, the village of Uimon, on the banks of the Katuna, where they formed a separate colony consisting of a hundred and twenty-nine men, and a hundred and thirty-five women.

About that time (1863) they were visited by M. Printz,[2] who found them a thriving people;

[2] From whose article in the Zapisky of the Russian Geogra-

they tilled the soil, kept bees, reared cattle, and
hunted wild animals, some were wealthy, and
owned five hundred horses, fifty or seventy head
of cattle, and a couple of hundred sheep, which
they kept exclusively for their own use. They
hunted in the Bukhtarminsk district, and on the
Upper Katuna, where the best sables are procured.
In former years the fur industry was more productive throughout the Altai than it is now, and
many more of the inhabitants of Uimon engaged
in it. As the population increased in the hilly
districts, the number of wild animals rapidly
diminished, and obliged many of the hunters to
seek other means of livelihood.

From Uimon M. Printz crossed the Katuna, and
ascending its left bank, reached the village of
Koksa, standing on the river of that name, and
inhabited exclusively by native Siberians,[3] who
were settled here in 1829 at their own request.
They had become thoroughly Russianized, and
retained scarcely any trace of their original type;
their style of living is somewhat inferior to the
peasants of Uimon, of whom they spoke in dis-
paraging terms, characterizing them and their
Bukhtarminsk brethren as vagrants or *varnaks*.[4]

phical Society we have derived these particulars of the
Kamenshiki.

   [3] The population of Siberia before the Russians came there,
consisted principally of Yakutes, Ostiaks, and Samoyédes.

   [4] Varnak is a common expression in Siberia, applied to exiles
and convicts. The word is derived from the Tartar *varanmak*,

Between the Koksa, which flows into the Katuna,
and the Bukhtarma, which joins the Irtysh, lies
the Holsun range forming part of the Altai system,
from which it is separated on the east by the
valley of the Katuna, whilst on the west it merges
in the lofty Koksun and Turgussun Bielki[5] (snowy
or white) mountains. Its height is between 5800
and 7200 feet, and its loftiest peaks form a kind of
table-land, such as are frequently met with in the
Altai. The road across the Holsun range from
the valley of the Koksa to that of the Bukhtarma
is very little known, and M. Printz had considerable difficulty in finding a guide able to show him
the way, but at last one was found and a start
made. From the bank of the Koksa the road
leads directly to the Katuna, and up this river for
ten miles; a ridge of rocks has then to be crossed
before the road enters the meadows by the side of
the Katuna, which it leaves shortly before the
latter is joined by the Ayulla, ascending the last-
mentioned river for a couple of miles to its confluence with the Kaitanak. This region is auri-
ferous, and M. Printz found a party of gold-
seekers prospecting the locality, but gold at that
time had not been discovered. From the head
waters of the Kaitanak he crossed a lofty pass to

signifying the passive state of an individual, as when he makes
a compulsory journey.

[5] For explanation of the term " bielok," or "bielki," as applied
to mountains in Siberia, see post, p. 230.

the sources of the Uimonsky-Biriuksa, which flows out of a small lake, and entered a region overgrown with birch underwood, the sides of the surrounding mountains being adorned with cedars and firs. This is a very difficult part of the journey, a narrow path encumbered with fallen trees leads through the forest to the summit of the Kaitanak, and it was late at night before the party reached the sources of the Biriuksa.

On these expeditions it is usual for the guides to choose the most cheerful spots for the encampment, whence the traveller may enjoy extensive and delightful views, but here there was no choice, a dense forest shut them in on every side, and no distant views were possible; the most that could be done was to find an open space near some stream, pitch the tent here, tether the horses, and prepare tea and supper; the latter consisted of pieces of mutton roasted on a spit, and kasha or porridge made of millet. After having refreshed themselves, they sat awhile round the dying embers, calculating the distance they had come, and how far they had still to go. The Cossack who accompanied M. Printz whiled away the time in teaching Russsian to the Kalmuks of the party, making them repeat after him different words, till at their absurd pronunciation and mistakes the laughter was loud and long, and the woods resounded with the general merriment. The guide, who had from

boyhood gone hunting in the *taiga*,[6] recounted
many of his adventures; he said it was not unusual
to encounter bears, and that he was once travelling
with the ispravnik[7] from Bukhtarma to Koksa,
when suddenly he saw one close by. This was
his first experience of these animals, and his in-
clination to kill it was so strong, that, forgetting
he was unarmed, he threw himself on the bear
with nothing but a whip. Fortunately another
peasant had observed the encounter, and levelling
his rifle as the bear was on the point of charging,
he fired and killed it. The pluck of the peasants
of these mountain villages is remarkable, the
Kamenshiki in particular seem not to know what
fear is.[8] It is not unusual to find men among
them who have engaged bears single-handed, and
an old man was pointed out to M. Printz who had
killed his eighty bears in single fight. The next
day they had to cross the last and loftiest of the
passes over the Holsun range. Descending the
Uimon Biriuksa to its junction with the Tiha
(slow) Biriuksa, they began the ascent of the

---

[6] "Taiga" is another Siberian expression. In Northern
Siberia it refers to the belt of uninhabited forest bordering on
the moss bogs which extend to the glacial ocean. In the Altai
it means the mountains where squirrels, and other animals hunted
for the sake of their fir, abound.

[7] The Ispravnik is the police-officer of the district.

[8] This fearlessness is a characteristic of the Starovertsi. In
the north of European Russia I have known peasants, armed
only with an axe, attack and kill these formidable foes.

latter. Vegetation gradually ceased as they
advanced, first the cedars disappeared, then the
pine forests, dwarf ash and birch only remaining,
while the summit itself was quite bare. The toil-
some ascent lasted more than a day; they were
amply rewarded, however, by the grandeur of the
view which unrolled itself before them. From
this, the most elevated part of the Holsun, the
whole mountain range could be seen, dividing the
waters of the two great rivers, the Obi and the
Irtysh. On the south a precipitous descent led to
the valley of the Bukhtarma, whilst to the north
the ground fell in terraces to the valleys of the
Koksa and Katuna. Near the sources of the
latter rose majestically the Katuna pillars standing in sharp outline against the pale blue of the
sky, while beyond the Bukhtarma glittered the
snowy belts of the Narym Bielki mountains.

The descent grew steeper and more steep as
they approached the Chernovoi or black water.
Fortunately the path was dry, and the weather
fine; had it been rainy, the difficulties would have
been greatly augmented, for the natives say that
hardly any horse will breast the ascent if it be
slippery.

After resting a few hours on the banks of the
Chernovoi, they pursued their way down through
underwood denser than anything one can imagine.
Branches of various kinds of trees and bushes
completely blocked the road in places, rendering

it necessary to force a way through them, protecting the face from their blows as they rebounded. The grass was higher than a horse, and so thick that it was difficult to ride through. Canes and *Heracleum*,[9] especially the former, were seen half as high again as a man on horseback. In a word, the southern slopes of the Holsun, well sheltered from the north, teem with luxuriant vegetation, contrasting in a marked degree with those on the north. Amongst bushes may be mentioned the guelder rose and common elder, never seen on the northern side, wild currant and raspberry in profusion; and amongst flowers, pinks and hollyhocks. The very colour and density of the verdure betoken a different nature, whilst countless swarms of butterflies fill the air.

The road or pathway descends by the Chernovoi to its confluence with the Bukhtarma, but to avoid the precipitous cliffs which press upon the river, it is necessary to ford it twenty times, a matter of no little difficulty near its mouth, owing

---

[9] Probably *Heracleum Sibiricum*, about which Gmelin informs us that the inhabitants of Kamchatka, about the beginning of July, collect the foot-stalks of the radical leaves, and after peeling off the rind, which is very acrid, dry them separately in the sun, and then, tying them in bundles, lay them up carefully in the shade in bags; in this state they are covered with a yellow efflorescence, tasting like liquorice; this being shaken off, is eaten as a great delicacy. From the stalks thus prepared and fermented with bilberries, the Russians distil an ardent spirit, which Gmelin says is more agreeable to the taste than spirits made from corn. (Loudon's Plants.)

to the depth of water, now and then above the saddle-girths, and the rapid stream. Vegetation here is as rank as it is on the Upper Chernovoi.

Along this and most of the smaller affluents of the Bukhtarma are stationed apiaries, at one of which M. Printz took a guide as far as the Bukhtarma, who told him that the bee-culture had greatly fallen off in recent years, owing to a mortality among the bees in 1859 and 1860, when he had lost most of his, having only thirty hives left out of 300.

The change from the wild, uninhabited, mountainous country, through which M. Printz and his party had been wandering for more than a month, to the highly cultivated fields on the Bukhtarma, where the rye grew as high as a man, and scented the air with its bloom, was most welcome to them.

The Bukhtarma here flows in a wide and picturesque valley, its stream is about 350 feet wide, and has numerous islands in it. On the left the mountains approach close to the water's edge, whilst on the right, with the exception of a few places, they are some distance off, the interval being filled in with corn-fields and meadow-land. These mountains are almost treeless, but they are clothed with a short grass, and they look far more attractive than the slopes on the other side of the Holsun range.

Descending the Bukhtarma, the first settlement

reached is Sennoi, on its right bank, eight miles
from the mouth of the Chernovoi, with a population of 177 men and 192 women, a place of some
importance. It has a church, hardly ever attended, a priest of the orthodox faith, whose
duties are almost exclusively limited to performing
the marriage service,[1] a Government inspector,
who is stationed here to look after the restless
inhabitants of this and the neighbouring villages,
and a mayor, whose functions apparently consist
in doing the honours of the place to the few casual
visitors who make their way into this remote part
of the world.

To this functionary M. Printz had recourse to
supply him with carts to take him and his baggage
to the next village. But after a diligent search
had been instituted, only one vehicle fit for use
could be found in the whole place, the fact being

[1] The Starovertsi of Bukhtarminsk belong to the old-fashioned
dissenters of the priestless sect, and have therefore no priests of
their own. In 1859 a clergyman was appointed to the district,
and the foundations of a church laid, which was consecrated in
1862. But the natives rarely enter it, and the congregation
on Christmas Day does not exceed twenty persons, including
the family of the Government inspector. On ordinary Church
festivals the clergyman has the church to himself. Nothing but
necessity drives them to the orthodox faith before marriage,
when they are obliged to sign a written engagement never to
return to the " raskol." This, however, they do not observe,
for they say that it was obtained by compulsion, and that its
object was to make the marriage tie more binding. They never
bring their children to be baptized, or fulfil any of the observances of the orthodox religion.

that people here always ride, and make use of pack-horses as a means of transport.

From the village of Sennoi it is ten miles to Verkh Narymsk or Ognevoi, beyond which the road is not worn for carts, and the steep ascents make riding the best mode of travelling. Between the last-mentioned village and Korobikha (eight miles), a high range has to be crossed, dividing the right tributaries of the Narym from the left affluents of the Bukhtarma. The pass is called "Bielok," a name applied by the natives to all the high mountains, not that they are perpetually snow-covered, but because the snow appears earlier and lies later on them than elsewhere.

From Korobikha the road follows the right bank of the Bukhtarma to Petcheh, or Upper Bukhtarminsk (ten miles), where the valley again widens out and is very beautiful, the village nestling in a hollow, at the foot of some terraced mountains.

On the east lie the Listviajny, or Larch mountains, forming the southern boundary of the Holsun range.

Through this range the Bielaya and Fikalka wind their courses. The first takes its rise in the Maral or deers' lake, high up in the mountains, and swelled by numerous feeders, flows with a good stream past the village of the same name, joining the Bukhtarma six miles from the village of Verkhny Bukhtarminsk; the Fikalka also flows past a village of that name, ten miles beyond

Bielaya, 4000 feet above sea-level. This is the furthermost Russian village in the direction of the Chinese frontier.

The volost or district of Bukhtarma, according to a recent return, has a population of 750 women and 668 men (304 of whom are able-bodied workmen), inhabiting eight villages, four of which are on the Bukhtarma itself. The land is very productive, and is reckoned the best in the Government of Tomsk, especially round the settlements of the Kamenshiki.

Though the inhabitants still speak of their country as " the Rock," the scenery in which their present abodes are situated is far from rocky, and very different from the cliffs and recesses where their ancestors hid. When these latter received the Imperial amnesty, and abandoned their inaccessible retreats, they settled in the open where the villages now stand, and where they found every requisite for a sedentary life. An inexhaustibly rich soil, a warm climate, fuel and water in abundance, and pasturage for their cattle. All kinds of corn ripen here,[1] and buckwheat is indigenous, though in quality not inferior to the cultivated grain. Vegetables are also successfully grown.

Bukhtarma is noted for the quantity and quality of its honey. Before the great mortality in 1860

---

[1] Even at Fikalka, notwithstanding its height, owing to its sheltered position, and the warm winds from the Kirghiz steppes on the south.

destroyed such numbers of bees, it was not unusual
to find proprietors of a thousand hives, and it was
in those days considered a more profitable invest-
ment than tillage. But this is not the case now,
and many who kept bees have taken to agriculture. There is no regular market for the disposal
of this honey, but merchants from Omsk annually
visit Sennoi towards the 15th August, or Feast of
the Assumption, almost expressly to buy that and
the beeswax, which is collected by that time, from
the other villages. About the beginning of September, rafts laden with these products are floated
down the Bukhtarma and Irtysh to Omsk.

The heat in summer in the valley of the Bukhtarma is usually sultry, and all fruits ripen early ;
melons and water-melons grow out of doors, and
strawberries, currants, raspberries, gooseberries,
and mountain ash are plentiful. The most characteristic of the flowers are the willow herb
(*Epilobium angustifolium*), wormwood (*Artemisia
absinthium*), clematis (*C. integrifolia*), lily (*Lilium
martagon*), globe-flower (*Trollius Asiaticus*), and
cow-parsnip (*Heracleum barbatum*). The most
conspicuous bushes are the honeysuckle (*Lonicera
tartarica*), wild jasmine (*Daphne altaica*), and
dwarf almond (*Amygdalus nana*). But the favourite occupation of the inhabitants of Bukhtarma,
and one for which they appear to have a natural
taste, is trapping wild animals. For this purpose
they build huts high up on the smaller affluents

of the Bukhtarma and Upper Katuna, where they
live in autumn and part of winter for several
consecutive weeks. They are so devoted to this
pursuit that they willingly sacrifice the comforts
of home life for the privations and hardships
incident to that of a trapper. In summer they
hunt deer and wild goats, hiring Kirghiz labourers
to attend to their farms and pasture their herds,
during their absence from home.

The best fur districts, particularly for sables,
are on the Upper Katuna and Bukhtarma and
their tributaries. These animals are caught in
traps or nets, and dogs are specially trained to
kill them, that the fur may be injured as little as
possible; for this reason guns are dispensed with
except where absolutely necessary. The sable
frequents the stony slopes of wooded mountains,
generally near the summits, descending at night to
seek its prey, and not returning to its nest before
morning. The method of snaring it is somewhat
peculiar, and may be described as follows:—The
trappers pass the night at the foot of the mountain where they expect to find sable, and almost
before daybreak commence the ascent, looking
everywhere for its tracks. As soon as these are
discovered the dogs are let loose. When the men
catch sight of the animal they endeavour to prevent its running up hill, for if it once get safely
back to its burrow, no power on earth can dislodge
it. They try and turn it therefore if possible

towards a neighbouring hill; but if in the meanwhile the dogs have tree'd it, they are obliged to
shoot it with the gun. More often, however, it
takes refuge on an exposed hill-side, which the
trappers immediately surround with their nets,
propping these up on sticks, and ballasting the
bottom with stones. The baffled animal now tries
to escape observation by crouching underneath
the net, whereupon its pursuers light a fire and
smoke it out. It then throws itself against the
top of the net, which it drags down from its
slender supports, and entangles itself in the
meshes. Fifteen men usually club together for
this branch of industry, and have one general net
about a thousand feet long, and standing four feet
high from the ground. It is one of the most
difficult as it is the most profitable of industries,
every sable skin being worth on an average
fifteen rubles. They hunt the fox and wolf in
autumn on horseback with dogs. Another source
of gain to the inhabitants is keeping tame deer,
which are caught young and brought up by
hand. By the third year the horns are a good
size, and are then cut off, and sent to China for
sale. The inhabitants of Bukhtarminsk, who
sprang from forefathers belonging to no particular
class in society, and coming from places widely
apart, have no distinctive type. But the freedom
of their existence, the nature of their occupations,
and of the region they inhabit, and above all their
inborn dispositions, impart to many a peculiarly

daring and expressive cast of features. Their
love of a vagabond life and adventure, inherited
from the early settlers, is preserved down to the
present day. As their ancestors came to seek the
"Bielovodiye," so are they ever in search of it
now. In 1865 a party of sixty men and women
crossed the Chinese frontier bound for the promised land, of which their traditions spoke; but
after two years of fruitless wanderings on the
confines of Russia and China, during which they
underwent every imaginable hardship and suffering, they almost all returned, some by themselves,
others escorted by Chinese. They had not hesi-
tated to sacrifice all their belongings, and some
were well off, for the sake of their religious con-
victions, and to satisfy their longing for freedom,
which, handed down from father to son, is ever
kept alive among them, and is so strongly
implanted in their nature that no loss or failure
can eradicate it. Not long ago, as we have seen
(supra, p. 77), a party of them, doubtless impelled
by the same restless cravings after their traditional
"white waters," or "white mountains," [1] visited
Lob-nor. Yet if we consider the solitary lives most
of these people lead—in winter in the great silent
forests for weeks and months together, engaged in
the all-absorbing chase, in summer by their apiaries

---

[1] Bielovodiye, country of white waters (from *biely*, white,
and *voda*, water). Bielogoriye, i. e. white mountain (*gora*,
mountain), is another name applied by Starovertsi to their
"promised land."

on the banks of streams, we cannot be surprised that their thoughts should take a serious turn, and that they should look to something better than to become units in the great empire from which they have so often tried to sever themselves.

As the tide of Russian civilization slowly but surely advances, threatening to swallow them up in their retreats, and compelling them to move farther and farther away in search of that unknown land, we can imagine them saying in the words of the Phocæans of Horace,—

Nos manet oceanus circumvagus : arva, beata
Petamus arva, divites et insulas.

The story we have endeavoured briefly to sketch of the Starovertsi of Siberia finds its reflex on the other side of the Atlantic. There, too, we find outlawed communities, such as the Mormons, the Shakers, and others, of whom Mr. Hepworth Dixon gave us a description some years ago in his "New America," choosing to dwell in out-of-the-way nooks and corners of the States, distinguished by many qualities which would fit them for citizenship, yet preferring to cut themselves off from society in order that they may practise their religious or irreligious rites far from the scoffing eyes of their fellow-men.

The analogy holds good in many points, in others again it will not apply. But it is singular that in name at all events there should be some similarity between the Mormons of the Rocky Mountains and the poor Kamenshiki or People of the Rock.

INDEX.

A.

C.

U.

THE END.

Lightning Source UK Ltd.
Milton Keynes UK
UKHW040704291122
413053UK00001B/99